Anna-Lucia Mackay is ⟨ intelligence. We have seen Circles, where the most successful captains of industry and some of the biggest sceptics, stopped, listened and were completely engaged and inspired by what she had to say. Her insights and understanding of emotional intelligence, and the impact of mindsets and how they are integral to anyone's success will benefit all who read this wonderful and inspiring book.

—**John Karagounis**, Managing Director and CEO,
The CEO Circle

Anna-Lucia's approach to cultural and people programmes always mixes great strategy with outstanding execution. A book that provides an overview of Anna-Lucia's approach to people and performance is an invaluable tool for any manager.

—**Ciaran Davis**, CEO Magazine's CEO of the
Year (2014), CEO, Australian Radio Network

Technology and the transparency it brings to leadership makes all of the elements in this book so poignant. Anna-Lucia has successfully distilled the key elements of modern day commercial leadership into a practical guide that all senior executives, managers and professionals should read.

—**David Baxby**, CEO, Global Blue, and
former Co-CEO, Virgin Group

I've had the great fortune to engage Anna-Lucia over the last decade and credit her with helping build a high-performance culture and in so doing driving up the value of my businesses when they are sold. This book is essential reading for every business, regardless of size.

—**Tim Eustace**, Chairman and Owner,
Mercury Private

Anna-Lucia seems to have a sixth sense for understanding people and performance and now this book shows us how she does it! This book is a must read for new, aspiring and experienced leaders.

—**Margaret Blunden**, CEO,
Grosvenor Financial Services Group

Anna-Lucia is the first and last person I would go to for advice, coaching and organisational training on EI. I have worked with her for 14 years and in that time I have seen her tools and coaching enable good leaders to become great, and strong leaders to become highly effective. Most of all I've seen leaders get really connected with what it takes to be Emotionally Intelligent. Now, all of this brilliant thinking is in *The Four Mindsets*.

—**Peter Lumsdaine**, CEO, O'Brien Group

All of our leaders and aspiring leaders have had training and coaching through HCM Global and Anna-Lucia. Why may you ask? Because they have been able to consistently improve the leadership qualities among the group which has led to increased longevity of employment of both managers and their teams; an increased motivation and passion for work; and a better sense of wellbeing and contentment for each staff member personally.

—**Scott C. Small**, Managing Director, Spinifex Holdings

Anna-Lucia Mackay has partnered with Nestlé Australia Ltd for the past 8 years and her style and use of the four mindsets approach in conducting the programs has significantly helped us build employee capability. The feedback from the programs consistently shows that Anna-Lucia's approach truly engages participants and helps them to take their learning back to their role for immediate application.

—**Garth Byrne**, Learning and Development Manager, Oceania Nestlé

While this book focusses on the role of the manager, this knowledge is heavily relevant to everyone looking for personal growth and development and in particular for those wishing to build and retain great quality relationships in any part of their life. A great reference tool for all.

—**Rebecca Sharp**, Learning and Development Manager, Australia and New Zealand, Merlin Entertainments PLC

As the business world of today keeps evolving and changing, so do requirements for those who want to be game changers in the business arena. Anna Lucia's book summarises key traits needed to be relevant today as a manager, leader, and most importantly influencer. *The Four Mindsets* is definitely one of the best books I have read this year on people management as it focuses on leadership traits so often overlooked. They are the ones that create the safe and open ended environment so many people today are looking for when they choose which organisation they want to be a part of.

—**Nikola Milivojevic**, CEO and President, Beauti Control, Tupperware Brands Corporation USA

Anna-Lucia is a high performance coach who has helped both aspiring and experienced leaders in our organisation adapt to an ever-changing business environment. Her training and indeed this book enables you to view your leadership style through a different lens and to achieve meaningful results irrespective of where your journey begins.

—**Deb Loveridge**, Managing Director Asia Pacific, Randstad, Singapore

Finally, a business book that offers pragmatic, thought provoking and insightful tools and methodologies that address the required skills and behaviours of a successful leader. All will benefit from reading this book and applying the skills, whether a new manager embarking on the leadership journey or an experienced manager who wants to reconnect with their team.

—**Nicola Griffin**, Sales and Marketing Academy Manager, Medtronic PLC, Middle East and Africa

One of the keys to good management is emotional intelligence and Anna-Lucia is working with us to help our Law Society members understand this by really connecting and motivating people—which is exactly what you'll find in this book *The Four Mindsets*.

—**Una Doyle**, Head of Professional Development, The Law Society

In early 2000 I asked Anna-Lucia to make an independent assessment on, not just how my direct reports felt, but how all the staff felt. The result floored me. In essence the majority of the staff felt unappreciated, a lack of confidence to make a decision, no communication on how they fit it to the goals of the organisation, and expectations about their accountability were unrealistic. So...Toss in the towel?...No way! So I engaged Anna-Lucia to start at the top, which included me, on what we needed to improve on. Within several years we had been nominated for industry awards, but more importantly, the team received the 'Best Team Award' for client service and proactive resolution within the Commonwealth Bank of Australia . The lessons learnt led to sustainable turnaround and growth.

—**Kevin O'Sullivan**, Former General Manager, Financial Markets Operations, Commonwealth Bank of Australia

Accomplished corporate consultant and executive coach, Anna-Lucia Mackay, presents another well-thought-out tool to assist new and aspiring managers to come to grips with the challenges of their roles. I can see this fast becoming a handbook for our new managers and complementing the excellent high-potentials mentoring program and other targeted leadership development programs that Anna-Lucia has delivered for us.

—**Kirti Jacobs**, Director, HR, APRA AMCOS

My belief is that being a manager is not about power, it's actually far from it. It's about being a positive influencer and enabler built on a foundation of respect, sincerity, consistency and authenticity. These values are at the core of Anna-Lucia's training and the four mindsets she's identified. The time I spent with Anna-Lucia gave me the confidence to stay true to my own beliefs and values as a manager yet have the tools and framework to navigate my way through unfamiliar and sometimes confronting situations with personnel.

—**Kate Willbourn**, Twitter Australia

The Four
MINDSETS

The Four MINDSETS

How to

INFLUENCE

MOTIVATE AND LEAD

HIGH PERFORMANCE TEAMS

ANNA-LUCIA MACKAY

WILEY

First published in 2015 by John Wiley & Sons Australia, Ltd
42 McDougall St, Milton Qld 4064
Office also in Melbourne

Typeset in 12/13.5pt Bembo Std

© HCM Global Pty Ltd 2015

The moral rights of the author have been asserted

National Library of Australia Cataloguing-in-Publication data:

Creator:	Mackay, Anna-Lucia, author.
Title:	The Four Mindsets: how to influence, motivate and lead high performance teams / Anna-Lucia Mackay.
ISBN:	9780730324782 (pbk.)
	9780730324799 (ebook)
Notes:	Includes index.
Subjects:	Management.
	Leadership.
	Employee motivation.
	Personnel management.
Dewey Number:	658

Cover design by Wiley

10 9 8 7 6 5 4 3 2 1

Disclaimer

The material in this publication is of the nature of general comment only, and neither purports nor intends to be advice. Readers should not act on the basis of any matter in this publication without considering (and if appropriate, taking) professional advice with due regard to their own particular circumstances. The author and publisher expressly disclaim all and any liability to any person, whether a purchaser of this publication or not, in respect of anything and of the consequences of anything done or omitted to be done by any such person in reliance, whether whole or partial, upon the whole or any part of the contents of this publication.

Contents

ix

About the author

Anna-Lucia Mackay is Group Managing Director of HCM Global and Career Crowd®, an award winning management consulting, training, coaching and mentoring company.

At 24 Anna-Lucia delivered her first management class at Manchester University on Motivation—the topic which would be the catalyst for a future career dedicated to understanding the links between people and performance, organisation and human behaviour.

Over the course of a diverse career, Anna-Lucia has consulted, trained and coached professionals, managers and executives in global corporations based in Europe, North America, the Middle East, Australia and Asia. Her diverse industry experience includes banking and finance, advertising, entertainment, education, engineering and construction, government, healthcare, mining and resources, not for profit, pharmaceutical and medical devices, telecommunications, human resources, luxury goods, and retail.

Since 2001, Anna-Lucia has designed, built and established three learning businesses and today is a leading educator, speaker and commentator in the field of management, adult learning and emotional intelligence.

With this highly unique combination of entrepreneurial, business and education skills Anna-Lucia has been recognised for her work and contribution to the fields of management and education through numerous National Industry Awards, including most recently as a finalist for the prestigious Telstra Business Women's Awards in Australia in 2012.

Anna-Lucia is married to William, and they currently live in Sydney with their twin boys — Hugo and Sebastian.

Acknowledgements

This book is a result of all the knowledge, opportunities and experiences afforded to me by wonderful people from all aspects of my life. Everyone has played a part in getting me to this point in my career and I thank you all.

In particular, I am eternally grateful to my mother and father for their love and support, and for preparing me as a child for life and for my future career ahead.

My husband, William, for your deep love and support, and for helping me gain the courage to continually step out of my comfort zone — knowing you are there to back me every step of the way as we travel this journey together. I love you so very much. Thank you.

My boys, Hugo and Sebastian, for your love, laughter and cheekiness which makes me smile every day and motivates me to do the very best job I can so I may be a good role model to you both.

My brothers Justin and Adam for your love and support, for continually challenging my thinking over the years and for being wonderful friends to me.

My friends from all aspects of my life for your love and support and for sharing your life, thoughts and learning with me along the way.

My staff and consultants over the years. I am so grateful for your input, friendship, work and help.

My clients for believing in me and entrusting your people and businesses to me. I love working with you all and thank you for that opportunity.

My chief editor, Geoff Bartlett, for helping me through the years, and for giving me the courage to write a book! I look forward to sharing this next part of the journey with you.

Wiley Publishing — my new friends, Lucy, Chris, Jem, Peter, Ingrid and Dylan — thank you for believing in me and for all of your help. It is so much appreciated.

Preface

The Four Mindsets: How to Influence, Motivate and Lead High Performance Teams is the result of 25 years of work and research in the field of management.

In the course of my career in management consulting and adult education, I have experienced two defining moments. The first came in 1998 when I read the article 'What makes a leader?' by the writer and psychologist Daniel Goleman, in which he examined what differentiates a star performer from an average performer.

The second moment occurred while I was attending a conference about 10 years later, when a speaker declared, 'Leaders must impact the thoughts, feelings and performance of their people'.

It seemed to me the second moment answered the question asked by the first!

When you strip away the ever-increasing complexities of leadership, how people think and feel about their leader at work will almost always determine the level of performance they achieve.

I taught my first management class in 1992—the subject was motivation—and since then I have been consumed by the challenge of understanding what makes people tick and what triggers people to achieve their known or hidden potential ... or not.

Over the years I have had the privilege of interviewing, coaching and teaching managers and executives working in a very broad range of national and international companies and organisations based in Europe, North America, the Middle East, Asia and Australia.

My companies HCM Global and Career Crowd® have worked with more than 100 organisations, ranging from leading multinationals who sit in the top five in their fields, to medium to small businesses, start-ups, government departments and not-for-profit organisations.

My teams and I have gained direct feedback from more than 10 000 people in a range of settings, from one-on-one interviews and coaching and mentoring sessions to small-team and large-team training sessions, seminars, webinars and conferences, in organisations representing most industries, including:

- advertising
- direct selling
- education
- engineering
- entertainment
- finance and banking
- FMCG
- food and beverage
- government
- health services
- human resources
- insurance
- luxury goods
- manufacturing
- mining and resources
- news and media
- professional services
- recruitment
- retail
- transport.

Our work has been rigorously assessed by third-party national industry bodies in the context of numerous prestigious awards programs. We have received frequent recognition for our achievements in helping Fortune 500 companies improve results through best practice learning, development and growth strategies for managers, executives and high potentials.

Our consistent research goal has been to identify indicators, patterns, trends and formula to help crack the code for what it takes to be the most effective manager and to answer the question: How do you influence, motivate and lead a high performance team?

We have tried and tested a combination of skills and techniques proven to help all managers increase performance and potential within their teams. These techniques have assisted organisations to improve performance and helped win awards for CEOs, department heads and teams in many industries.

We have evaluated many of the best management tools currently used around the world. This book will share with you some of the tools we believe are invaluable in helping managers understand what makes people tick and how to manage them in order to build and sustain a high-performing team.

In the following pages I share what we have learned in 25 years and applied over the past 12 years. Each area of knowledge has been incorporated into our award-winning strategies for the creation of centres of excellence, turnaround and culture change programs, and employee engagement initiatives that underpin the increased productivity and profits of a variety of industries.

Since 2007 HCM Global and Career Crowd® have had the opportunity to observe and dissect the dynamics of high performers and those who are not, and have identified and documented the triggers for high performance at work for both individuals and teams.

From more than 5000 surveys, performance assessments, one-on-one interviews and 12-month case studies, we have found that, when activated correctly, these triggers influence employees and team members to perform at their highest level for sustained periods of time. The result is that they often achieve things they had previously not thought possible.

In short, we have found that the triggers point to four crucial mindsets that are critical to bringing about high performance. These mindsets are based on four core feelings that are generated by people's thoughts, observations, assumptions, perceptions and beliefs about the person who leads them.

The impact of the line manager on a team's performance has long been understood. It has often been said that 'people join organisations but leave their leaders'. There is more to it than this, though.

High-performing managers recognise the importance of understanding what makes people tick, and this book is written to help you do this. We will share with you:

- what high-performing managers focus their minds on
- what they actually do
- what they do *not* do.

We identify the factors that are most significant for building strong connections with individuals and teams, and that, in turn, trigger high performance and the realisation of high potential—known or hidden.

I sincerely hope you find this book a valuable resource in your own quest for performance excellence.

How to use this book

The Four Mindsets has been written as a multipurpose tool to help CEOs, leaders, human resources professionals, management consultants, coaches and training professionals to coach, mentor or train managers, team leaders and future leaders to achieve high performance.

Designed to accelerate learning in order to activate the high performance mindset in both managers and employees, this book explores:

- what makes people tick
- how management, motivations and mindsets have changed
- the mindset and triggers of high-performing employees today
- the mindset required by managers and team leaders today
- how to create the desire in people to perform at a higher level
- how to become an engaging leader
- how to unlock hidden potential

- the role of the psychological contract

- how to unlock discretional effort.

We share 12 years of experience working with Fortune 500 companies and award-winning strategies for the creation of centres of excellence, turnaround and culture change programs, and employee engagement initiatives that underpin increased productivity revenue and profits in a variety of industries.

The High Performance Mindset Model™ is the focus of this book and has been designed as a learning pathway when coaching, training and mentoring in a variety of settings, including team meetings, corporate book clubs, one-on-one sessions, small-group training sessions and webinar discussions.

Based on adult learning principles to assist *learning, retention* and *knowledge transfer* in your workplace, each chapter contains:

- a knowledge section outlining easily understood best practice concepts that are the most up-to-date and relevant today

- a full summary reviewing the key processes and ideas discussed for reinforcement and 'on the job' learning

- reflective questions for personal or group use

- suggestions for where to start in applying the strategies introduced in the chapter.

For more resources and practical tips to help you manage, coach and mentor your people to reach the highest levels of performance, go to www.fourmindsets.com.

Introduction

Before we begin to turn to the Four Mindsets™, it's important that we understand a few common concepts that underpin learning in this book. These relate to the *psychological contract*, the changing management landscape today and the concept of a *mindset*.

The psychological contract — what is it and why is it so important?

Every manager should understand the concept of the psychological contract. This unwritten contract has the ability to enhance, or destroy, everything you do. It's all about people and, as a manager, everything you do should relate to people!

To understand the psychological contract, let's first look at what we mean by 'contract'.

A contract is simply an agreement made between two parties. Contracts are usually formal, requiring a signature, and state clearly what needs to be done or agreed to. For example, an employment contract lists the intentions and expectations of both employee and employer. It is a formal, signed document.

A psychological contract is also concerned with intentions and expectations between parties but is not formal. Rather, it is based on people's perceptions that typically relate to the give and take (or informal negotiations) between two individuals—issues surrounding what is right and wrong, how people should work together, what is fair and what is not, loyalty and trust.

The psychological contract is far more powerful than the employment contract. The employment contract will not unlock potential and high performance, whereas the psychological contract will do exactly this because it is based on *thoughts*, *feelings* and *emotions*, and more often than not the *desire* to go over and above expectations—often referred to as *discretional effort*. The agreement is, as Denise Rousseau puts it, 'implicit, involving an individual's beliefs of reciprocal exchange between two parties pertaining to trust, loyalty and the well-being of all involved'.

Importantly, the psychological contract relies on commitments by both parties as it is based on very significant human behaviours that can help build a relationship or break it in an instant.

Psychological contracts are typically focused on ensuring that the employee and the organisation share understandings so they can work together to achieve mutual goals. To accomplish this, a manager needs to understand their team's perceptions of them in terms of their obligations to their team, their personal behaviour, how they deal with staff and others, and the quality of their work.

The key here is that managers must accept that reality in itself is *not* enough; it must be demonstrated to, and perceived by, your people.

For example, a manager may believe they are fair in their dealings with staff, and indeed they may be. Most managers, however, would not be conscious of being *seen* to be fair; they would simply hope others would think this of them.

But a manager needs to understand that the *perception* of fairness in the workplace is a hot button for most people. For example, when an employee feels their manager is not fair, it will more often than not break the psychological contract. This, in turn, kills the employee's desire to go over and above expectations, shutting down discretional effort, which is so often the very thing required for the achievement of sustained high performance.

When the psychological contract is broken, it usually comes down to managers:

- not understanding that they need to manage both tasks *and people*

- not understanding the impact they have on their team's thoughts and feelings

- being promoted into their roles without the sincere desire to help others

- being promoted into their roles without the necessary people skills

- lacking in self-awareness

- lacking in empathy

- not understanding what makes people tick

- not understanding that they are tasked with the responsibility to coach and mentor

- favouring some people over others

- being deemed not to be trustworthy, fair or consistent.

Often when the contract breaks it has nothing to do with tasks, competence, technology, policies, practices, procedures or products. Yet most of an organisation's time is spent in these task-focused areas. The bottom line is that people may feel discomfort but they can live with these things if the people factors are in place.

When the people factors are overlooked, their discomfort grows and resilience starts to diminish, triggering varying degrees of disengagement and disconnection. Left unchecked, this can escalate to acts of aggression, passive or active withdrawal, acts of sabotage such as petty theft, or the formation of team alliances—all of which can undermine the manager or organisation.

There are many psychological contracts in play in our lives. Outside of work, we have them with our parents, siblings and friends. In each instance there are implicit expectations and an element of give and take. Similarly, at work we have psychological contracts with clients, peers, other departments, suppliers and employees.

Understand that the strength of the psychological contract is determined by the quality of the relationship you have with people, and at times this will absolutely override what is written in any formal contract.

This is your first crucial step to understanding what makes your people tick.

Management today — how has it changed?

The factors that powered the high performance mindset 20 years ago are significantly different from those that operate today. Most managers would not even be aware of this, let alone be able to describe how it is different and why.

When we asked what managers are focused on and concerned with each day, fewer than 10 per cent mentioned anything to do with how their people think and feel. Most expressed deep frustration with being charged with the responsibility of shaping their team's *thinking* and *feelings*, with most saying, 'Why don't people just do their jobs?'

But let's take a closer look at this.

First, the reason why the management techniques of 20 years ago are still relevant today is that many people in your workforce—the baby boomers and older Gen Xers—will have passed their formative working years during this time. What this means is that their mindsets were formed (and, for some, 'set') during a very different time—and therein lies the problem.

Those arriving in the workplace in the 21st century have a very different mindset and set of beliefs about work. What work means to them is the reason why they don't 'just do their job'.

We are currently caught between two significantly different work and management eras. During the first, ending around the early 1990s, a worker would be told what to do and would do it, usually without question and with little, if any, collaboration. A manager gave orders, respect was expected and given, and title and status were formal and significant. In this era, the working world was *task focused*, authoritarian and hierarchical, and not particularly *people focused*. It was an era when information was *not* shared openly.

The second era, in which we work now, is one where open communication and collaboration are the norm. Everything is open to question and discussion, everyone's views are taken into consideration, hierarchy is limited, status is becoming less important, work and family life overlap, nothing is permanent, there are no guarantees and feedback is expected.

Unsurprisingly there is tension and misunderstanding between the generations, and Gen Y is getting a bad rap! The irony here is that the managers who find it hardest to cope with Gen Y at work are from the generation that parented them—that is, they are the very people who taught them to question everything and that they could do anything!

What we must understand is that in today's (more affluent) western world most people's basic needs are met, and their desire to satisfy other, more individual needs has made management much more complex. People today need to understand more about why and how work will meet their needs and correspond to their values and belief systems.

This notion is very new to most managers and requires a shift in mindset from what they have previously experienced, observed or been taught. In fact, the roles of managers and of leaders are merging. Research shows that managers and team leaders who run productive and engaged teams increasingly do the work of 'leaders' too. It is no longer enough to ensure that jobs get done. All levels of managers are now becoming more responsible for displaying those attributes formerly associated only with leaders.

These attributes include getting people on board, selling the organisation's values and vision, and communicating and connecting with people in a way not previously expected of managers. For those whose management focus has been firmly fixed on task, strategy and execution, this represents a significant change in how they think and operate.

So if the roles of managers and leaders are merging, then it would make sense that influence within organisations is shifting and changing too. Ask yourself who has the biggest influence in the workplace today. Is it the CEO, the senior management team, middle management, the HR team or people department?

Now ask yourself these questions:

- Who is closest to the front line?
- Who is closest to the most people?
- Who talks most to the people on the front line?
- Who is closest to the customer experience?
- Who is still delivering to the customer directly?

Our research showed that the high performance mindset is created *on the front line* with the person at the *lowest* level of management.

The team leader

The high performance mindset of your people along with the organisational performance and potential are unlocked *or blocked* by your team leaders through their conscious or unconscious behaviour. Yet typically they are the group in your organisation given the least investment and support.

The CEO, senior leadership team, middle management and HR should act as their support team. These groups should be focused on providing the tools, support, direction, coaching, mentoring, training and growth opportunities that team leaders need.

The reality is that the most senior managers get this level of support, as may middle managers if they are lucky, but not the team leaders. Yet they have the closest contact with the people and processes that actually produce most of the organisation's results.

The filter effect

Why is it that the CEO, senior managers and often the middle managers have the least influence? The reason is the filter effect.

Typically in organisations, the CEO and senior leadership team devise the strategies for improving performance—assessing customer requirements, updating technology and performance measures and so on. At this point, one of five things will happen:

1. The CEO will accept all the recommendations put forward by the senior leadership team.

2. The CEO will accept some of the recommendations put forward.

3. The CEO will reject some of the recommendations and accept others.

4. The CEO will implement their own strategy.

5. A combination of points 3 and 4 will be implemented.

This means that on many occasions the CEO will need to 'sell' a number of new strategies to the senior leadership team. As a result, this team will start to apply a set of conscious and subconscious judgements, assumptions and filters to the information. This behaviour is driven by basic human emotions that range from excitement and enthusiasm to indifference, confusion, resentment and insecurity.

In other words, the very people who will be implementing the strategies are starting to form mindsets that will either drive or hinder them.

Let's now assume that the CEO has empowered the senior leadership team to brief the middle managers on the new strategies. Sure, the CEO will also help drive the messages (some do it well, some not so well), but given today's management environment of supposed 'empowerment', it is the senior leadership team who will do 90 per cent of the communication to 'sell' the message to the next level down.

At that stage a second series of filters will be applied, and the original information and its intention will now be diluted further. The process will then take place at the level below (the supervisor level) with the same result. Finally, the supervisors will inform their team leaders.

It is only at this point that the team leader will pass on the information, if they feel confident to do so. Often they don't and instead rely on the monthly CEO update to the staff (if available) to make the impact required.

If you don't believe me, you have surely heard the refrain 'Don't ask me, I'm just the messenger', or 'I don't know why, just do it!' or even 'That's senior management for you'! You might also do a quick comparative study of the following:

- What percentage of time is spent directly briefing the lowest level of team leader, as opposed to the senior leadership team and management team?

- What percentage of the training budget is spent on developing, supporting, coaching and mentoring the higher echelons of management versus the team leaders?

- How much time does the CEO spend with the team closest to the front line?

- After the strategies change, how much time is spent with the team leaders to help them with ongoing implementation over the following 12 months?

- Who in the organisation receives the highest level of change management training?

- What forum do you provide for feedback from this group?

In most organisations we have worked with, the answers are almost never in favour of the team leader. The reality is, *the intention of the CEO does not arrive intact on the front line.*

It is important to recognise that your team leaders are 'closer' to your people than you are in terms of frequency of contact and are likely to be more socially connected (electronically and personally) with them. Through continuous observation and conversation they know more about what makes their team tick and have gained a wealth of knowledge about each individual team member. They are also closer to 'what it takes' to actually do the job (many are still doing it *and* managing at the same time).

But, just like everyone who has played a part in passing the information down to your team leaders, the team leaders will also apply a filter—either consciously or subconsciously enabling or blocking your strategies, but this time on the front line.

When implementing new strategies, the CEO and HR team must work in unison to overcome this and make time to influence the team leaders directly rather than always relying on others to do this for them.

It is absolutely essential that the team leaders are not last in the chain—and on the receiving end of filtered, diluted and misinterpreted information. So in order to give your frontline staff the best chance of achieving a high performance mindset you must ensure your team leaders themselves have a high performance mindset.

How do we develop our team leaders (and in fact all levels of management) from here?

First, they do need to be task competent. If you have incompetent people who lack the technical skills to do their job, you must ask yourself why they are incompetent and do they know they are incompetent? Are they capable of attaining competence? Do they want to and will they put in the effort? How long will it take them to achieve competence, and how will you support them?

Given that most organisations do quite well to ensure they have task-competent managers and team leaders with the right technical skills to do their jobs, it then comes down to mindsets.

The impact of mindsets

The high performance mindset is crucial, and every manager and team leader should adopt it. You first need to understand that the high performance mindset comprises four crucial mindsets, all of which are underpinned and driven by the team leader's or manager's understanding of what does (and does not) motivate people and human behaviour.

Most people are wired more or less the same way. How they think and feel translates into how they go about their work and how they go about their day, which in turn helps shape their mindset. A mindset triggers behaviours and actions in a person and it is these behaviours and actions that generate results, whether good or bad, average or exceptional.

So exactly what is a mindset? A simple definition is 'a way of thinking that determines a person's behaviour, outlook and attitude'.

Managers must focus on influencing the thoughts and feelings of their team in order to enhance their performance. How your people think and feel will determine how they go about their work, how engaged they are and how committed they are to you, the organisation and their goals. So managing their mindsets from the moment they join your team or organisation is imperative.

To do this, you need to understand a few things about mindsets.

Mindsets are generated over time and are either conscious (a person chooses a particular mindset) or unconscious (the mindset develops instinctively as a response to a stimulus, such as a change of procedures). But while people sometimes don't consciously choose a particular mindset, it can easily build up over time and become the norm. Equally, mindsets can change in an instant.

Mindsets are influenced by a person's beliefs, assumptions and perceptions (which do not always conform to reality). A conscious mindset is often driven by a desire and is required to reach a goal—even one previously believed to be unattainable. A conscious mindset is more often than not required to realise potential (known or hidden). It often takes cognitive strength to override thoughts, feelings and emotions that act as a barrier to realising goals.

The high performance manager has a way of thinking that means they *consciously and purposefully choose behaviours and actions or activities* to directly influence how people think and feel *before* they think about how their people perform and *sustain* that performance.

The four crucial mindsets

Each of the four crucial mindsets—the Emotional Intelligence Mindset, the Connection Mindset, the Growth Mindset and the Performance Mindset—is critical to increasing performance and productivity in employees and strengthening the psychological contract.

How to achieve each mindset and how they come together are the subject of this book. The right mindsets to create and activate high performance managers and team members are represented in figure A.

Figure A: the High Performance Mindset Model™

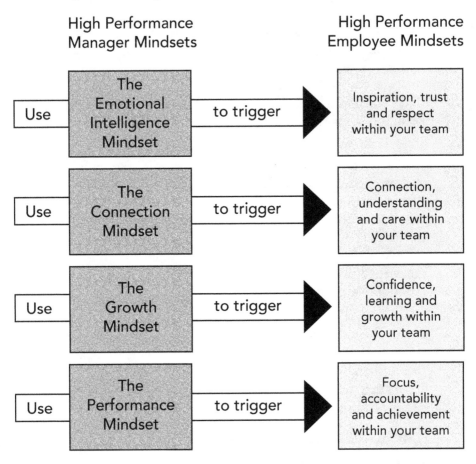

Part I

The Emotional Intelligence Mindset

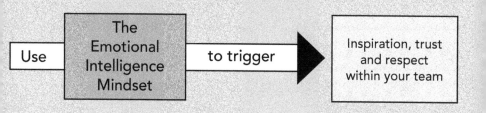

| Use | The Emotional Intelligence Mindset | to trigger | Inspiration, trust and respect within your team |

In this Part:

➤ The manager as role model—the key to influence

➤ How to develop emotional intelligence:
Step 1—self-awareness

➤ How to develop emotional intelligence:
Step 2—self-management

➤ How to build trust

chapter 1

The manager as role model — the key to influence

One of the most successful ways to influence people and raise performance in the workplace is for every manager to adopt the mindset of a role model. As Peter Drucker, author of *Management Challenges for the 21st Century*, has said, 'People do what they see'. Just as children mimic the behaviour, actions and attitudes of their parents, employees look to their managers and leaders.

In the workplace, as in life, we find positive and negative role models. People copy people! Simple examples of this are the use of bad language and non-adherence to a dress code. It is interesting to note how often someone who dresses and speaks in a certain way when they first join the team will within six months have adapted their language and dress to match those of other team members or the leader.

After years of asking people at work who their role models are, and *why*, we have found there is a clear trend in the traits and characteristics defined and articulated. These we classify as conscious traits (traits that people can define and articulate).

However, there are also subconscious traits — traits that people are impacted by but are unaware of. These subconscious traits can include how a person presents themselves and how they speak, behave and act, all of which create a subconscious impression in others.

When was the last time you thought about yourself as a role model?

For most, not recently enough. If you want to influence how people think, feel and perform, you must become a role model — and make this a consistent and conscious mindset. This is not something that should be left to just happen. Those managers we interviewed who were considered by others to be role models understand this and actively work to control the perceptions others have of them.

In his book *Moments of Truth*, Jan Carlson describes how the perceptions others have of us are shaped by such 'moments of truth'.

According to this theory, each moment of truth will affect, on a conscious or subconscious level, the way you are perceived. This, in turn, affects performance in the workplace — either positively or negatively. In other words, people are continually making conscious or unconscious judgements about you, your team, business or organisation and the way you work based purely on what they *perceive* you to do or not do. The facts have nothing to do with it!

Organisations who score the highest in terms of culture have managers who are conscious role models. They are taught how to role model and how to influence their staff to activate high performance. They also carefully control and monitor the perceptions others have of them.

During our research high-performing employees were asked if they felt their manager was a positive role model and, if so, what traits had the biggest influence and impact on their personal performance.

Regardless of industry, job function and status, the most common traits were consistency, a caring nature, authenticity (a sincere and genuine person), a good communicator, results oriented, and a desire to help and develop others. The first three components are summarised on the following pages and resurface throughout the book. The other components, mentioned again and again in a variety of contexts by the top performers surveyed, have sections of this book dedicated to them.

Consistency

Although a variety of words and phrases were used to describe this trait, the core finding was that a manager who behaved inconsistently and was unpredictable *severely and gravely* impacted high-performing team members and the overall performance of their team in a negative way.

The research showed that high performance requires an element of goodwill, and there is high correlation between goodwill and predictability. This also forms the basis of the strong psychological contract outlined in the introduction.

A consistent and predictable manager means staff are not 'on edge', wondering what mood their manager is in and whether it is safe to tell them something or ask for help. Recent history tells us that many corporate collapses stem from the inability or unwillingness of team members to share knowledge with their managers for fear of what it could lead to.

Your team needs to feel safe with you. This is *not* about keeping them in their comfort zone and not challenging them; it is about making it safe for people to share the knowledge you need in *all* situations—good or bad.

As a role model, you should always adopt a philosophy of 'no surprises' in any situation. Your people must trust you to respond logically and rationally when pushed to the edge.

That is not to say you must always be happy. Your responses should be congruent with the specific situation, but a positive role model will always manage to apply a rational, non-threatening approach in the face of any adversity so they can deal with the problem and then move on.

A caring nature

This is a highly significant trait that people (and high performers in particular) look for in their role models and managers in business today. It is not a quality you are likely to learn about on any leadership course or at business school, but you will find that the word comes up time and time again in statements such as 'They should take better care of us', 'They just don't care' or 'My manager doesn't care'.

Followers need their leaders, managers and role models to genuinely care—*and to demonstrate* this care—for their people. Employee engagement surveys consistently attest to this. Having a caring manager is now becoming a prerequisite for successful management, which has had a major impact on evolving management theory.

Managers who are perceived not to care about their people will not fully engage their teams, and without this engagement, higher levels of performance will rarely be achieved or sustained over the longer term.

Our research also shows that it is the high performers who are most often overlooked. Managers tend to believe that everything is okay with them as they are doing so well. But your high performers *must* feel they matter to you *as people* and not simply for the revenue they generate or the skills they bring to the table.

Think about it: how would your people rate you?

Authenticity and sincerity

If you are not perceived to be authentic and sincere, everything you do will be affected. This trait underpins most positive role models. A manager who is believed to be insincere will not activate high performance in their team. When a manager or organisation is deemed to be insincere or inauthentic, watch the staff turn over and performance plummet.

Here is a typical example drawn from one of our surveys. A senior manager was perceived to be authentic and sincere—that is, until a client he had worked with regularly outside of the company got a job as a manager inside the organisation. Now reporting to this senior manager, the former client shared how disappointed and disillusioned she was and how she had been 'totally taken in' by this person. In simple terms, now she was on the inside, she saw a different persona from the one the senior manager presented to clients outside the office. Now she perceived him to be 'fake'. She quickly left the organisation.

People will not tolerate any form of 'fakeness' in today's workplace and will most certainly move on, often even with no job to go to, as this is how strongly they feel.

In today's workplace people increasingly need to find a way to mesh their personal values with those of their organisation *and their manager*. As a result, if a manager's values are not deemed to be authentic and sincere, the relationship between the organisation and the individual will not survive. We will discuss this more in the following chapters.

In summary, the 'manager as role model' approach wins every time.

Chapter summary

- Employees will mimic the behaviour, actions and attitudes of their managers, so lead by example.

- The research clearly shows that high performance requires an element of goodwill, and there is a high correlation between goodwill and a manager's consistency and predictability.

- A manager who is considered a positive role model by their team has the following traits:

  - management consistency

  - a caring nature

  - authenticity, sincerity and genuineness

  - a positive attitude

  - a desire to help and develop others.

- Your high performers *must* feel that they matter to you more *as people* than for the revenue they generate or the skill they bring to the table.

- If you are not perceived by your staff to be authentic and sincere, everything you do will be affected.

- Organisations that score highest in terms of culture have managers who are conscious role models.

- Your team needs to feel safe with you so they will share the information you need to know in all situations — good or bad. You must respond logically and rationally.

- People increasingly want to mesh their personal values with those of their organisation *and their manager*. If a manager's values are not deemed to be authentic and sincere, the relationship between the organisation and the individual will not survive.

- A manager modelling poor behaviours, attitudes and actions is giving 'permission' for others around them to do the same.

- To be a good role model you must be self-aware. In understanding your impact on others, you must understand how you present yourself (intentionally or not).

Reflective questions

1. What evidence is there that people are copying you for the wrong or the right reasons?

2. Provide two examples of how you have demonstrated predictable behaviour in the past week.

3. How often do you get frustrated and irritated with your staff?

4. Would your staff describe you as someone who gets frustrated and irritated?

5. Do you truly 'care' for your staff? How much? (Rate yourself out of 10.)

6. How do you think your staff would score you (out of 10)?

7. Do you need to be cared for at work?

8. If you answered no, do you think this impacts your desire to care for others?

9. How do you actively show that you care for your staff?

10. Would your high performers say they matter to you *as people*? How do you know? Provide examples.

11. Provide a recent example of how you demonstrated sincerity.

12. Provide examples of your authenticity at work.

Where to start

1. Identify the key influencers and role models that have played a part in your life so far; if you don't have any, consider that too.

2. Study these role models and consider what they may indicate about yourself. How similar or different are they from the role model traits described here?

3. Do this exercise with your team and identify the common themes. Assess any differences between the traits they nominate as important in their role models and the traits you show.

chapter 2

How to develop emotional intelligence: Step 1—self-awareness

Research shows that a high level of self-awareness is fast becoming the number one skill required in the workplace by managers, leaders and high performers. Regardless of your industry, title or job description, if you are not self-aware, it is unlikely you will reach and sustain high levels of performance as a manager, realise your true potential or be able to help others in your team to do the same.

Self-awareness is commonly believed to be the cornerstone of emotional intelligence. Anyone charged with the responsibility of increasing performance levels and managing others must learn what it takes to become emotionally intelligent. And your starting point is self-awareness.

What does it mean to be 'emotionally intelligent'? In *Working with Emotional Intelligence*, Daniel Goleman describes emotional intelligence as 'the capacity for recognising our own feelings and those of others, for motivating ourselves, and for managing emotions well in ourselves and in our relationships'. The idea has played a significant role in changing how people manage in today's workplaces and businesses. What complicates things is that this shift in management thinking is ongoing and many managers are still caught in the middle of the transition.

Traditionally a manager's role was seen as being 'task based' and was measured primarily by the quality of their decision making, strategy application and task execution. Today these skills account for *less than half* of the job! The top-performing managers in today's workplace focus more than 50 per cent of their time on people-based activities, where caring, collaboration and gaining buy-in are the goals.

In simple terms, it's about the way in which you manage and conduct yourself and how you manage your interactions with others each day. Those who score high in emotional intelligence competencies seem to have one thing in common: they continually seek to understand why they behave, react and respond in the ways they do. And using this knowledge, they try to better understand the behaviour of others.

With this self-awareness mindset comes the ability to predict the likely response in others *and consequently prepare for it*. In most cases, it is this ability that distinguishes those who are highly emotionally intelligent from those who are not.

Common sense would tell us that this ability to anticipate and prepare for potentially tricky or negative events would be a key skill of a successful manager. Research shows that managers who are not skilled in this area will typically become frustrated, regretting their knee-jerk reactions and then having to deal with the fallout rather than focusing on 'value adding' activities.

So how do managers do this in the heat of the moment?

Four out of five managers said they first spend time understanding their own pressure points — their hot and cold buttons — so that when they are pushed, they are psychologically prepared to respond in a way that focuses on finding a solution.

Most of the time, we already know how most people are going to respond to a conversation or a situation. What these high performers show is that you need only 'choose' to activate the appropriate mindset—which requires self-awareness and a certain amount of discipline—and then act on it.

For example, think about a recent negative encounter with a family member or team member. Now, looking back on the situation, you will see that of course they were going to say the things they did or react in the way they did. This is because past behaviour is still the best predictor of future behaviour. This is one of the most important things you can learn in understanding the mindsets of other people and what makes them tick!

An emotionally intelligent manager is constantly looking for the cues that people give through their actions, responses, body language and tone of voice. This information helps a manager to manage their people more effectively, both as a team and as individuals.

For some managers this is second nature; for others, it is a choice they must actively make. Many managers who are caught up in the busyness of their days do not pick up on this vital information and therefore miss out on the opportunity to use it later on, particularly in situations relating to performance and feedback (what Ken Blanchard calls 'the breakfast of champions').

So how do we learn to interpret the clues and signals people give us? This brings us back to self-awareness, and your first step is to develop your *own* self-awareness. To be self-aware is to have a clear perception of your personality, motivations, responses, behaviours, emotions, habits and thoughts.

The connection between thoughts, feelings and behaviours has long been recognised, but to reflect, observe and consider this continually is key to developing your emotional intelligence. By considering each of these components, you will begin to build up a picture of what makes you tick—and what brings out the best (and worst) in you.

Self- or emotional-awareness, suggests Daniel Goleman in *Working with Emotional Intelligence*, is the ability to recognise 'one's emotions and their effects'. People with this competency, he says:

- know which emotions they are feeling and why

- realise the links between their feelings and what they think, do and say

- recognise how their feelings affect their performance

- have a guiding awareness of their values and goals.

You will see that much of this is about *thoughts, feelings* and *performance*. To understand these competencies in more detail, let's consider the simple example of how hunger can affect mood. The behaviour of people who feel hungry may affect those around them. They may speak more bluntly than usual or be more short tempered; at worst, they may become truly angry in a situation that doesn't warrant such a response.

Another example is tiredness. People who are overtired can be more emotionally sensitive. By being aware of this and knowing the possible consequences, you can choose a course of action to avoid a potential negative result.

A key area to explore in relation to self-awareness is the impact of perception on mindsets. Most people will have heard the saying 'perception is reality'. Whatever action you take in a given area, if others do not perceive it, then it may as well not have happened.

For example, you can tick all the right boxes in your own personal performance review by having done all the things expected of you, but if your people perceive you to be a poor manager and your performance as lacking, then your 'truth' is of little relevance.

The reality is that your team's level of performance directly correlates to how they perceive you, in terms of your values, needs, drives, skill level, management capability and personality traits—both at work and outside of work. So it makes sense that you would want to control how people perceive you by the actions you take and how you behave.

You should also be aware that today's workforce is much more interested in *who* their managers and leaders are as people and *what* they stand for—inside and outside work. This has a significant impact on their perception of you and *how* they perform for you.

If your team judge you to be a good manager and can relate to you as a person, then the strength of the psychological contract grows, and key performance drivers such as employee engagement, motivation and collaboration—as well as discretionary effort—increase. So to unlock your team's capacity and potential, you must influence how people think and feel about you, and this starts with self-awareness.

Another advantage of being self-aware is that this usually means you are able to make better choices and decisions in life. Self-aware people know what they need and what motivates them, and will look to address these factors. They are therefore generally more stable and content—a good starting point for any great manager.

The other major by-product of self-awareness is confidence.

Although we will discuss this trait in more detail later in the book, confidence is relevant here because of the direct correlation between self-awareness and confidence. People who are aware of their strengths and weaknesses and what motivates them are typically more confident in their capabilities—and more at peace with what they are not so good at. They then focus on improving what they are not so good at, which again serves to create a strong foundation for effective management and role modelling.

Chapter summary

- Self-awareness is becoming the number one recognised skill for managers and leaders in business today.

- Self-awareness is the cornerstone of emotional intelligence.

- Emotional intelligence 'is the capacity for recognising our own feelings and those of others, for motivating ourselves, and for managing emotions well in ourselves and in our relationships' (Daniel Goleman, *Working with Emotional Intelligence*).

- To be self-aware is to have a clear perception of your personality, motivations, responses, behaviours, emotions, habits and thoughts.

- Your team's level of performance directly correlates to how they perceive you in terms of your values, needs, drives, skill level, management capability and personality traits—at and outside of work.

- Regardless of any action you take in a given area, if others do not perceive what you do, it may as well have not happened.

- To unlock your team's capability and potential you must impact how people think and feel about you.

- If your team deem you to be a good manager and can relate to you as a person, then key performance drivers such as employee engagement, motivation and collaboration increase.

- An emotionally intelligent manager is constantly looking for the cues that people give through their actions, responses, body language and tone of voice. Having this information helps a manager to manage their people more effectively, both as a team and as individuals.

- An individual who is self-aware is able to make better choices and decisions in life. They know what they need and what motivates them.

Reflective questions

1. How do you think your team would describe you?

2. How would those close to you describe you?

3. What are the key differences between these descriptions?

4. How do you present yourself in meetings?

5. How do you come across in pressure situations?

6. How do people know when you are uncomfortable—what do they see?

7. What do people not know about you?

8. How do you know that you don't have any blind spots (things that others see that you don't)?

9. What are your core values in life?

10. What are your top three needs in life?

11. What are your key motivators?

12. What upsets you most with other people?

13. What are your key management strengths?

14. What are the top three areas you need to work on?

15. What do others say you need to work on that you disagree with?

Where to start

1. **Self-analysis.** Think about what happens when you are at your best and at your worst. Try to connect the dots. What is at play? Use the reflective questions provided to help you gain a better perspective on yourself.

2. **Get feedback.** Think about how you can collect information about what people think and perceive about you. Start by asking key people in your life to give you honest feedback. Refer to performance reviews, client feedback and customer references. Perhaps even take a 360 degree assessment such as the Emotional and Social Competency Inventory (ESCI), which I highly recommend.

3. **Sit back and watch yourself in action!** Analyse your behaviour, thoughts and responses during the next meeting. Choose a meeting where it is safe to say less and listen more. Then just watch and listen to yourself and see what you can't help but say, feel or think. This will tell you a lot about your hot buttons!

4. **Babysit!** If you are a parent, or if you sometimes care for children for long periods, analyse what you say to the children when they are playing up. See if there are any clues here as to your needs and values.

chapter 3

How to develop emotional intelligence: Step 2—self-management

Self-management describes how we manage our emotions, responses and behaviours and how we control and manage their impact on others day by day. In relation to emotional intelligence this is a 'must have' competency. We need to be able to manage ourselves whenever we're stressed or our buttons are pushed. This is typically a core trait of any positive role model at work.

The work environment requires dealing constantly with people, problems and money. The ability to self-manage effectively makes the difference between achieving results and not! The research shows that if this competency is missing, then significant problems occur that are usually far reaching and highly destructive to productivity and organisations.

From our interviews with many managers, it became evident that high performers, whether managers or frontline staff, scored highly in two key areas: self-control (how people control themselves and their reactions in negative situations) and resilience (how people bounce back from negative situations).

Self-control

To build skills in self-control, it's necessary to understand what is happening in difficult situations. To be able to do this, it's important to understand human behaviour and how it is impacted by:

- *your physical state.* This is your actual physical being—your actions, body language and behaviours.

- *your emotional state.* This is how you feel. We all feel many emotions, and some of them are going to help us be our best, while others will hinder our performance and our ability to maintain self-control. Knowing how you are feeling, what you are feeling and why you might feel a certain way is crucial to self-control.

- *your psychological state.* This is what you are thinking, what you believe to be the case and what you spend time reflecting on. Your thoughts also will either help or hinder your ability to maintain self-control. You should therefore build awareness of what you are thinking about—and in what direction this thinking takes you.

Knowing the way you need to express yourself physically, understanding your emotional state, and thinking and acting on useful thoughts are what is required to self-manage.

This rational thinking is often what's missing when people give way to emotional outbursts, when the part of the brain responsible for rational and logical thinking is not activated, but instead the emotional part of the brain takes over and the body goes into 'fight or flight' mode.

So to self-manage effectively, a person needs discipline and a strong mindset to overcome the urge to respond emotionally rather than rationally. It means managing disruptive emotions and physiological impulses in order to focus clearly on the problem or person in question. In the words of Lao Tzu, 'The best fighter is never angry'! Any disruptive emotion that could cloud judgement should be removed. The goal is to achieve the best possible result so the problem does not persist or worsen.

The hard part is that often it means putting aside your own feelings and thoughts in order to look at longer term benefits. Many people struggle with this, as it's far more satisfying to surrender to your immediate feelings for the sake of short-term reward.

What do we need to do to increase our self-control? Daniel Goleman in *Working with Emotional Intelligence* defines self-control as 'managing disruptive emotions and impulses'. This requires that we, as Goleman says:

- manage [our] impulsive feelings and distressing emotions well

- stay composed, positive and unflappable, even in trying moments

- think clearly and stay focused under pressure.

Achieving these competencies requires discipline, the mental strength not to be sidetracked, the ability to override the daily speed bumps we encounter and to stay focused on the end game.

So how do we manage this?

Much has been written on this. In extreme circumstances, of course, an increasing number of people resort to therapy and medication to help them gain greater control over their feelings, impulses and emotions, and find a better balance in their life and work. We are not therapists; however, our research shows that those with a high level of self-control tend to exhibit the following five qualities.

They have a balanced perspective

Perspective can be defined as a particular attitude towards or way of regarding something. People who lack self-control can find it difficult to 'put things into perspective'. Typically, they find themselves exaggerating problems and situations. When this happens, it usually signals that they feel helpless and cannot achieve the result they are looking for. This, in turn, causes them to lose control of their emotions, which usually sets off a vicious circle.

Those with a balanced perspective, on the other hand, apply a disciplined approach, removing emotion from the mix, analysing situations and deciding what they can control and influence and what they cannot.

To better understand what this means, let's look at a well-known model, the 'Circle of Concern/Circle of Influence', as outlined in Stephen Covey's book *The 7 Habits of Highly Effective People*.

Covey's model identifies two components:

- things that I have control over (Circle of Concern)
- things I do not have control over (Circle of Influence).

For example, you can influence your family, co-workers, clients, team and so on. You cannot control what they do but, depending on your skills, you can influence them.

Anything outside of these two circles is not within your control and influence, so you should not waste time and energy trying to control it.

They are able to reframe situations

Again, those who score highest in this area are able to find a positive in a negative situation. This 'reframing' allows us to revise our views on any number of events and situations.

For example, a client rejects a proposal you submitted. On reflection, however, you realise it was a low-value proposal that was going to take up a lot of your time, whereas now you can spend time looking for more valuable clients.

They think about 'what's in it for me' (WIIFM)

Think through how a situation could get a whole lot worse for you, your team or a team member if you don't react in a reasonable way. Often taking the time to reflect on the possible outcomes of a situation can help you maintain your self-control.

They are able to depersonalise

A person exercising self-control often tries to give the benefit of the doubt. People do and say the strangest things—sometimes you just don't know what is going on in someone's head. When a person responds in way that is not usual for them, think to yourself, 'Something must be going on for this person to behave this way'. Don't immediately think this is a personal attack.

They prepare ahead of time for uncomfortable situations

It takes a degree of skill to get into the right mindset and one of the best things you can do is prepare ahead of time. You often know there is a strong likelihood that someone will push your buttons so thinking through how you are going to manage your response when they do will serve you well. You can also manage your feelings by biding your time before responding. Take a sip of water, for example, or ask a question. This measured response will help you retain your composure.

The key is to distance yourself from the emotion, plan your response and not get drawn in.

Resilience

Resilience is about being able to bounce back from hard times or challenging situations. As you would expect, self-control and resilience are closely correlated. That is to say, how you manage your emotions will directly influence how resilient you are — or become.

The more resilient you are, the better you will be at coping and at self-management. In addition, the more resilient you are, the more resilient your team will become, as your ability to weather storms and cope in tough times will directly influence the same capacities in your people. Remember, attitudes are contagious!

So let's examine the resilient mindset.

> Managers who demonstrate resilience typically:
>
> - believe in what they do and why they do it
> - understand that everything is down to them — they don't rely on others for their sense of self-worth or self-esteem
> - have realistic expectations of themselves, of others and of situations
> - are dedicated to health and wellbeing
> - are level-headed problem solvers and good decision makers

- recover from setbacks quickly without allowing situations to snowball

- manage their stresses privately

- know what would undo them and focus on ensuring that it does not happen

- know their limits and do not attempt to exceed them

- approach people and situations flexibly.

Managers who lack a resilient mindset typically:

- are prone to emotional outbursts

- can have dependencies

- can suffer stress-related ailments

- think in the short term rather than the long term

- are inward focused

- are not doing the job that is most suitable for them

- adopt a victim mentality.

The key to resilience is sustainability. There is no point driving yourself into the ground for short-term results if you then burn out and ruin relationships in the long term. This is no good for anyone—least of all you—and sets the wrong example. The resilient mindset requires you to treat your time in your role as a long race. It requires careful planning, pacing yourself, coaching, practice and building up endurance levels.

Following are the eight most common steps people take to build their resilience.

They simplify their lives

They know what has the greatest value to them in life. They remove both physical and psychological clutter and confusion.

And they understand what's really important, what their needs are and what their priorities are. This removes or reduces emotional distractions, fears and stumbling blocks.

They 'lighten up'

They do things that encourage them to take life less seriously. They find their inner child and encourage 'play', and they make time to spoil themselves with small treats such as a beach walk, playing with the children or nature activities.

They take command of their life

They take control of their thoughts, intentions, actions and deeds, recognising they do have choices. They develop healthy and positive thoughts. They look for the beauty in things, are grateful for what they have and do not focus on what they don't have.

They balance their lifestyle

Think about your lifestyle. Is this the way you would choose to live your life? How do you spend your time? What are your values and priorities? Is your lifestyle congruent with what's important to you? Measure your pace of living. Are you happy with your work–life balance?

They work to maintain their health

Think about your:

- *immune system.* Work to strengthen your immune system and rejuvenate your metabolism by eliminating physical and emotional toxins.

- *nutrition.* Follow a healthy eating plan to aid your body's healing powers and provide the fuel it needs. Eat smaller amounts of food at more regular intervals to improve digestion.

- *physical fitness.* Implement a regular exercise program and proper sleep regime to help build stamina and maintain energy levels. Use exercise as a release from emotional and physical stress.

They stay true to themselves

Stress signifies a lack of harmony between you and what is happening in your life. The first way to reduce your stress and anxiety levels is to ensure the job you have matches who you are as a person in terms of your personality type and the goals or purpose you have set yourself.

If you are doing a job that does not match this criterion, your stress levels will be higher than they should be. So you are unlikely to reach your true potential or sustain a high level of performance in the long run.

They understand what happiness is and isn't!

Happiness was traditionally promoted in western cultures as something that must be 'found' or something that comes to us when we change our circumstances—'I will be happy when I move house, have a baby, get married ...'. It has been demonstrated that achieving such objectives does not in itself generate long-term happiness. It does for a short time, but then other factors kick back in.

Positive psychology indicates that the key to happiness is *intentional activity*. Happiness is not out there to find—it's inside us! *Happiness is a mindset.* Research suggests that a person's propensity for happiness is determined 50 per cent genetically, 10 per cent through circumstances and 40 per cent through intentional activity.

So a major key to happiness is to take action! *Step 1:* Find the true source of your unhappiness. *Step 2:* Identify your strengths, talents and goals. *Step 3:* Identify what you need to do to *work* towards your new state.

They keep the right company

When facing challenges, balancing your time with different groups so you spend time with the right people is important. Divide your time appropriately between your family, work colleagues and friends.

Remember that when your resistance is low and your stress levels are high, your ability to control negative behaviour decreases, so it becomes even more important to be with the right people!

Chapter summary

- Top managers score very highly in the areas of self-control and resilience. Work to be able to bounce back from negative situations.

- Your behaviour is impacted by your physical state, your emotional state and your psychological state.

- Those who scored highly in controlling emotions:
  - ➤ have a balanced perspective
  - ➤ can reframe situations
  - ➤ think about the long-term effects
  - ➤ depersonalise
  - ➤ find a way to put a gap between their emotions and their response.

- Self-control and resilience are very closely correlated. So how you manage your emotions directly affects how resilient you are or become.

- The top five ways high performers build resilience are:
  - ➤ They don't overload themselves with emotional or physical clutter.
  - ➤ They find ways to lighten up their life.
  - ➤ They take control of what they can control and let go of things they can't.
  - ➤ They embrace a healthy and balanced lifestyle.
  - ➤ They are true to themselves and are doing a job that matches who they are as a person.

- You need to be able to manage yourself when you're stressed or when your buttons are pushed.

- A balanced perspective allows for a disciplined approach to removing emotion, analysing the current situation, and deciding what you can control and influence and what you cannot.

■ When a person responds in a way that is not usual for them, remind yourself that something may be going on for this person to behave this way, so it may not be a personal attack.

■ Distance yourself from any emotion in a conversation, and plan your response so you do not get drawn in.

■ Treat your time in your role as a long race. It requires careful planning, pacing yourself, coaching, practice and building up endurance levels.

Reflective questions

1. When was the last time you gave way to an emotional outburst? Why was this?

2. Would your team describe you as having high levels of emotional control?

3. Are you able to stay positive in difficult situations? Provide three examples.

4. Provide one example of when you had to balance your perspective in a situation in order to calm down before you reacted.

5. Provide an example of the last time you needed to reframe a situation.

6. Think of a recent occasion when you had to actively get into the right mindset to deal with a situation. Describe how you did it.

7. Provide an example of how your attitude immediately brought about a change in the attitude of those around you at work. What happened?

8. Have you actively simplified your life in recent times? If so, how?

9. What do you do to ensure you don't take life too seriously?

10. How well do you look after yourself (score out of 10)? Provide five examples.

11. Does your job enable you to be true to who you are? Discuss how.

12. How happy are you? What makes you unhappy?

13. How much of your time do you spend with family, friends and work colleagues? Discuss.

Where to start

1. Think about a meeting you have coming up with someone who presses your buttons. Prepare a mental plan on how you are going to maintain your cool and control without becoming emotional.

2. Look at your workflow, identify the pressure points and bottlenecks in the months ahead, and put a plan in place now to help you. Don't let the problems just creep up on you—this is how stress happens.

3. Identify a mentor or coach in your organisation who demonstrates self-management well and book a meeting with them to discuss how they do it.

4. Work to increase your awareness of your physical, emotional and psychological states, and what influences them.

chapter 4

How to build trust

Most people understand that successful relationships are built on a foundation of trust. Without trust, relationships typically break down through some form of conflict or avoidance behaviour by one or both parties. While trust can take years to build, it can be lost in a moment. With one word, one gesture, one action, a relationship can change forever, regardless of all the good that may have gone before. When it comes to trust, nothing is 'fair'.

As a manager, you must be conscious of what it takes to build trusting relationships at work. Unlike relationships outside of work, where trust with those with whom you *choose* to have a friendship or association builds over time, your work relationships are forced upon you (a bit like families!), so more care needs to be taken because the stakes are much higher. This can trigger heightened levels of emotion.

Personal vs professional trust

Let's look at trust in the workplace. First, it is important to establish that there are two types of trust at play—personal trust and professional trust. Personal trust is based on a person's character traits. Professional trust is based on work performance. Research shows that those managers who are the most successful at unlocking higher levels of performance and discretional effort in their teams exhibit both personal and professional trust.

It is important to note that if you manifest one type of trust, this does not mean you will necessarily display the other. More often than not, in fact, underperforming managers have one and not the other.

For example, you can implicitly trust a person based on their character traits, but the same trust may not apply in the workplace. In this case, those traits you trust that are displayed outside of work are for some reason missing in the workplace. Conversely, you may trust a person based on their work skills without trusting them personally.

For example, Simon was an IT executive sent to us by a major international bank for coaching. We were briefed that he was technically exceptional; however, morale in his team was low. Results and performance had dropped and wherever possible peers and managers chose not to associate with him.

When we talked to Simon's team and peers through a 360 degree review process, it became evident that his team totally trusted his abilities and problem-solving skills, but they were afraid of him because of the character traits he displayed day to day. These traits included overly aggressive language, stance and approach. Outside of work, however, he showed no aggression at all.

So think about it. What aspects of you do people trust or distrust? Do you exhibit both equally? To help you consider this, let's look at the most common traits found in those we researched who were considered to have earned high levels of personal trust.

> Typically, people told us that personal trust emerged as a result of the following top 10 character traits: (1) empathy, (2) putting self second, (3) being a 'good person', (4) working for the good of others, (5) selflessness, (6) being team spirited, (7) keeping their word, (8) adopting an open-minded approach, (9) being non-judgemental and (10) exhibiting an ability to build rapport.

Notice that the common theme is caring and working for the good of others and not putting themselves before their team.

Among those surveyed on professional trust, the following character traits were the most common: skill level, experience in the job, qualifications and accreditations, high IQ, technical competency, ability to execute and achieve work-based goals, success attained, decision-making ability, problem-solving ability and ability as communicator.

You will see that these professional trust builders are more obvious and less likely to change over time. Even with the surfacing of new generations and fads, competency is still and probably always will be essential! Based on the feedback given, it could be concluded that personal trust comes from emotional intelligence–based competencies, while professional trust is based on technical and IQ-type competencies.

Knowing and showing yourself

In today's workplaces managers are increasingly expected to share more of themselves and who they are *outside of work*. We touched on this 'self-disclosure' earlier. Twenty years ago, to reveal anything of your private life at work was seen as unprofessional; today it is becoming essential.

In their best-selling book *Why Should Anyone Be Led by You?*, authors Robert Goffee and Gareth Jones discuss this issue at length. Their key point is that it is critical for a leader today to *know* themselves and to *show* themselves. To achieve this, they emphasise the importance of self-awareness. Leaders must first be clear about how others perceive them, as well as opening up to show different aspects of who they are. Or as Goffee and Jones put it, 'Effective leaders must know enough and show enough to maximise their *leadership impact*'.

The implication here is that today people are unlikely to trust you, and therefore follow you, if they can't relate to you and understand you. Although this is becoming true of all age groups, it is younger people who will continue to drive this trend. Think about how social media are stimulating people's need to connect, to know what others are doing, what they're interested in, where they are, who they're with — and even what they are eating!

When people relate to you, they come to understand who you are and what makes you tick. This leads to trust. In visual terms:

Relate   Understand   Trust

For some, this level of transparency can be very confronting. There are many reasons for this. Some people don't like to mix work with personal matters and prefer to maintain a private life. Perhaps they don't think such information is relevant in the work context or they feel they don't have time. Some may simply be introverted or shy and don't believe they are interesting to other people. Others worry that by revealing too much they risk being judged.

Unfortunately, none of these reasons will prevent mistrust. If you are a closed book, people will become wary of you and will take much longer to open up to you. Worse still, they will create their own version of who they think you are, and you do not want this!

So let's look at what you can do to ensure your team can build their trust in you.

Your first job is to share what makes you tick, just in simple terms. Think about who you are as a person. Who are you literally (a mother, father, brother, aunt ...)? How did you get to where you are today? What are your values? What do you appreciate and why? What motivates you? What are your hobbies? What makes you laugh? What music do you like?

Recently I was speaking to someone about why she had chosen never to tell people at work that she loved to bake. She could not understand why this would be of interest to anyone, let alone why bringing in biscuits for her team could be fun. I eventually managed to persuade her, and the team could not believe it. She displayed such a hard edge at work that to visualise her 'baking' seemed absurd. It changed her team's perception of her overnight! Of course it took more than this one piece of information, but it was a mighty start!

So your starting point can be fairly straightforward and does not require you to share deeper aspects of who you are. Think about sharing the information you would at a dinner party with someone you have never met before — it's usually the lighthearted, surface things we share. Remember, your people are just human beings and want to communicate and share with you.

The final step in understanding trust is to grasp how all this links to how you operate as a manager — and as a role model.

The research shows that the fastest way to build high levels of trust is to choose, adopt and display the following mindsets of *transparency*, *acceptance*, *congruence* and *reliability*.

Transparency

People need to know who they are dealing with. They need to know exactly where they stand—and where you stand. Any uncertainty or ambiguity around this and fear rises and trust decreases. People need to feel you are being open and honest with them and not covering things up in any way.

In engagement surveys, one of the top five engagement drivers relates to people's need for a sense of being 'in on things'. More open and regular communication will serve to satisfy this need. People will understand that they can't know everything!

Transparency goes both ways too. You must seek feedback from your team. People *need* to feel they can share their thoughts with you, so they can be transparent with you too.

Acceptance

People need to be accepted and respected for who they are as individuals. As soon as they start to feel judged, insecurity creeps in and a range of negative behaviours starts to manifest.

With acceptance comes respect. As a manager, your people must feel and know that you respect them. They do not typically need you to agree with them all the time but they do need to feel heard without fear of criticism.

Finally, even if you feel a person does not deserve respect, you must deal with them courteously. Manage them quickly, efficiently and fairly for the sake of your other team members. (I have seen too many managers unable to show respect to those who cannot do the job or who are failing, which can often lead to claims of workplace bullying.)

Congruence

Probably the fastest way to erode trust in your team is for you to show a lack of congruence between what you say and do. Practising what you preach must be your mantra, as consistency is essential.

Nothing turns people off more than someone who is perceived as 'fake'. You must deal with people consistently, regardless of their title or position. There should never be one set of rules for some and a different set of rules for others.

Perceptions of your honesty and integrity lie within this area, so you must be sure not to send the wrong messages.

Reliability

The final area relates to your skill levels and your ability to deliver what you say you will. Those who consistently rate the highest in this trait are highly skilled, know what they are doing, are great problem solvers, hold themselves accountable and deliver on time. In other words, their team can count on them in every way. Most people would like to think they do all of this, but the reality is often *very* different.

This is the fastest way for you to shape positive opinions about you as a manager. Be aware, though, that this criterion can also be used by others just as fast to build up a negative opinion or perception of you. Commit to continually building your skills, keep up to date and be honest in what you can and can't deliver. Do all this and you will fulfil your role as a role model too!

Chapter summary

- There are two types of trust to build at work. Personal trust is based on character traits. Professional trust is based on work performance.

- Personal trust is based on emotional intelligence–based competencies, while professional trust is based on technical and IQ-type competencies.

- As a manager, your people must feel that you respect them. People do not typically need you to agree with them all the time, but they do need to feel they will be listened to without fear of heavy criticism.

- Be aware that exhibiting one type of trust does not mean you will necessarily exhibit the other.

- Ensure congruence. Your dealings with people must be consistent, regardless of who they are in terms of title or position. There should never be one set of rules for some and a different set for others.

- Be reliable. Deliver what you say you will.

- As a manager, you must be conscious of what it takes to build trusting relationships at work.

- Leaders must be clear about how others perceive them and open up to show different aspects of who they are to maximise their leadership impact.

- Commit to continually building your skills, keep up to date and be honest in what you can and can't deliver.

- To stay in the game, you have to adapt—and not judge!

Reflective questions

1. How do you consciously go about building trust in your team?

2. Would your team describe you as selfless?

3. Would your team describe you as 'a good person'?

4. Would your team members rate you higher for personal trust or professional trust?

5. How well do your team members relate to you?

6. Do you think they understand you as a person?

7. What would most of your team know about you personally?

8. Are you more of an introvert or an extrovert, and how much does this influence your level of disclosure?

9. Would your team feel that they are 'in on things' when it comes to what's going on with the organisation generally?

10. How naturally judgemental are you (scored out of 10)?

11. Would your team say your *skills* are reliable? Give examples.

12. How reliable are you in relation to delivering exactly what you say you will (scored out of 10)? Provide three examples from the past few days at work.

13. How well do you practise what you preach (scored out of 10)? Provide three examples from the last week.

Where to start

1. Socialise with your team. Go out with your team after work to a lighthearted setting and talk! Perhaps hold a barbecue in the park or at your house.

2. In your next training session or team meeting, build in an element of 'What you may not know about me'. Each member shares some information that they may not have shared before, perhaps about an interest or hobby. You could do this to get things flowing socially.

3. When you next meet with your team members individually, ask for feedback on how you can better manage them.

4. Based on the reflective questions, devise a strategy or checklist on what you are going to do in the next quarter to overcome your areas of weakness, then think about what you will consciously and actively demonstrate to your team.

Part II

The Connection Mindset

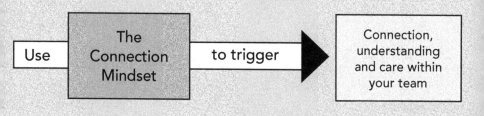

In this Part:

➤ Understanding what makes people tick and Learned Intuition™

➤ How to connect people to the business

➤ How to create a personal connection

➤ How to have a challenging conversation without breaking connection

chapter 5

Understanding what makes people tick and Learned Intuition™

Over the years people have often suggested that I have a 'sixth sense' for understanding people and situations. I have a sometimes uncanny ability to predict and anticipate, almost precisely, how people will behave, what they will say and even what they will be thinking in a situation.

Contrary to what most people think, this perceived sixth sense, or high level of intuition, is most of the time a result of data analysis and rational and logical thinking, *not* a gut feeling.

Most people believe that intuition is a trait that you either have a predisposition for or not; you were born with it—or not. Although there may be some truth in this, I believe intuition is an aptitude that simply requires a certain mindset, some basic skills and, perhaps most important, a *desire* to activate. I refer to this aptitude as Learned Intuition™.

To illustrate this theory, let's think about reality TV for a moment. How is it that we are able to predict the judges' comments and scores in a variety of situations on these shows? Most of us don't know how to sing, dance, dive or ice skate, so how is it that we can so often anticipate the scores the judges of such activities will give?

Even more crazily, we can do this for cooking shows where we cannot taste, smell or touch the food being judged! Then there are the dating and survival shows where in many cases it becomes quite obvious who is going to go next, or who is in love with whom, and even though we know the producers manipulate the events and personas presented, we can still see what is going to happen! This is Learned Intuition at play, not gut feel.

How are we doing this? Our rational, logical and analytical brain is firing on all cylinders. We are observing, monitoring, dissecting and analysing, consciously and unconsciously, every move, every gesture, every look, every breath, every word. We are picking up signals, patterns and trends that will suggest to us what is going to happen, and what the repercussions and knock-on effects are likely to be.

So why is it that many managers and leaders do not bring this level of insight to work, do not seem to understand the people with whom they work closely every day, and are so often surprised by how they behave?

There are a few reasons for this to do with skills, behaviours and mindsets. Some of them we have already discussed, and some we will cover in this part of the book.

Let's start with mindset. First, the mindset required is one that a manager or leader must *choose* in order to activate a deeper level of consciousness of what is going on around them at work and why.

The potential problem here is that for many managers, 'getting the job done' is the priority, so making this choice often requires a significant shift in mindset, which they believe will compromise their production goals. If a manager's priority is truly to get the job done efficiently and effectively, however, then dedicating more time to understanding their people is an essential part of the equation.

Having activated this mindset, it then comes down to a couple of steps that we have already covered: *self-awareness* and *self-management*.

As discussed in chapter 2, self-awareness is about understanding 'what makes you tick', which is the first step to understanding what makes others tick and developing intuition.

In chapter 3 we discussed self-management—and how to stay on track and manage potentially disruptive emotions. This is important here as there is a very strong relationship between being able to do this and understanding others—again necessary to developing intuition. As our case studies, research and common sense tell us, people who have less ability to self-manage and often lose control are more stressed. As your stress levels rise your ability to pick up signals and cues from others about what is going on diminishes.

Mindsets, self-awareness and self-management were covered in Part I of this book. Now we turn to the last critical skill required for Learned Intuition—empathy.

Empathy

In my view, empathy is the most underrated of all management competencies. Even the word is enough to put many people off; in fact, I have had clients who have asked me to change the word for something a bit more 'businesslike'!

So why is this word so divisive? The answer is that for many it conjures up negative images of 'warm and fuzzy' thinking by people who are more concerned with their employees' 'feelings' than with getting the job done! The truth, however, is quite different and corporations are now starting to see the real value of empathy and the benefits it can have for business.

Another reason is that many people misunderstand just what empathy means, confusing it with *sympathy*. So what is the difference? The Oxford Dictionary defines sympathy as relating to 'feelings of pity and sorrow for someone else's misfortune'; empathy is about being able to understand another person's perspective.

Think of empathy as sitting in the middle of a continuum between *apathy*, denoting a lack of interest in understanding how others feel or see things, and *sympathy*.

Apathy   Sympathy

Empathy

This perspective works well in business, where it is often important to find a happy medium between going too far and not far enough.

Daniel Goleman in *The Emotionally Intelligent Workplace* defines empathy as 'an astute awareness of others' emotions, concerns, and needs ... our understanding of others' feelings and concerns flows from awareness of our own feelings'.

Research from Goleman and the Hay Group found that people with this competence:

- 'are attentive to emotional cues and listen well

- show sensitivity and understand others' perspectives' (Goleman)

- adjust their behaviour to the social setting

- 'understand where a person's feelings are coming from and why

- are open to diversity.' (Hay Group)

The Hay Group describe those people who *do not* demonstrate this competence as follows:

- They see others primarily in terms of ethnic or other stereotypes.

- They misunderstand or are surprised by others' feelings or actions.

- They clash with others as they don't understand their concerns or thoughts, even if obvious.

While this gives us some clues as to what empathy looks like, it is also important to understand why it is so relevant in business.

> When interviewing top-performing executives who scored highly on empathy, we asked them how empathy helped them in business. Typical responses were as follows:
>
> - Empathy provides clues to what people want, need and value — all essential components to driving creativity, innovation and employee engagement.
>
> - Empathy drives connection between people, in turn driving the relationships required to sell what is created and innovated, be it a product or a concept.
>
> - Empathy is the difference between those who sell well and those who do not.
>
> - Empathy is the difference between those who deliver high levels of customer service and those who do not.
>
> - Empathy is at the root of all good relationships.
>
> - Empathy is about understanding how your customers see things.
>
> - Empathy is about understanding how your staff see things.

(continued)

- Empathy is about respecting others.

- Empathy is critical to persuasion and influence.

From these responses we can see that empathy is not only useful in business; it is *critical* to business. How can we possibly attract, engage and retain clients and employees without being able to see things from their perspective or understand their needs, motivators and drivers?

According to research conducted by the Emotional Intelligence Consortium, 'those with high levels of empathy will typically outperform those who are equally skilled but who are considered to be less empathetic'.

The following tips will help you hone these skills.

Tip 1: Ask questions and listen

Be interested in your team and get to know them as well as possible by asking their opinions on things and then *listening* to what they say. Listening is a key skill. There are two distinct types:

- Precision listening is listening for facts, figures and data.

- Empathetic listening is listening for what is going on behind the words being said—the thoughts, feelings, hidden messages and inferences.

Tip 2: Suspend judgement

Empathy requires you to understand how others see things, not to judge them. Those who are judgemental and who cannot keep an open mind will always struggle to empathise with others in a positive way. If the other person feels in any way disrespected or unsafe when dealing with you, they will start to shut down and hide things from you, and as a manager this is the last thing you want.

Tip 3: Learn more about human behaviour

As a manager, you need to understand the links between something happening and someone acting, as shown below.

Stimuli → Thinking → Feeling → Behaviour → Performance

Tip 4: The way people think, feel and behave can be a result of their beliefs

Much of a person's attitude and behaviour can stem from their belief system. This can be broken down as follows:

1. A belief is something you hold to be true or false, right or wrong.

2. Our beliefs are one of our most significant filters and can dramatically influence our behaviour.

3. Beliefs can come from the assumptions and judgements we make about ourselves and others.

4. Many of the limitations people face in life come about through their self-imposed beliefs.

5. You become what you believe you are.

In the words of Mark Twain, 'If you think you can, you can. If you think you can't, you're also right'. For example, you may have a team member who believes they are not 'creative'. This belief then negatively impacts their ability to be creative and generate ideas—it becomes a self-fulfilling prophecy.

Tip 5: The way people think, feel and behave can also be a result of their values

Here's what you should understand about values:

- Values are how we think things ought to be or how people ought to behave, especially in terms of qualities such as honesty, fairness, integrity and openness.

- A value is a measure of the worth we put on something or someone.

- Our values link directly with our purpose in life and our experience of it.

- The values we hold set a context for our experience in life.

- Our values determine what we feel is most important to us.

- A person can become aware of what they value when they experience a situation in which that value is absent. This then creates a strong negative emotion in them.

For example, if the values of a person at work are not aligned with their values outside work, then stress and conflict will arise. As a manager, you must help match your people's and the organisation's values. For example, if someone values empathy and caring for others, you must show how the organisation reflects these values by empathising and caring for clients and staff.

Tip 6: The way people think, feel and behave is also a consequence of their needs

Here's what you should understand about needs:

- Needs are the things and feelings a person must have to be minimally satisfied in life.

- People's needs can vary very widely.

- After food and shelter most people's needs are more often than not associated with feelings of safety, belonging, self-esteem and achievement of inner purpose.

- When a person has unmet needs, they are usually 'trapped' or 'hooked' by people, events and thoughts, and are more susceptible to becoming resentful, angry and in more extreme cases depressed.

- Needs are different from 'wants'. Needs relate to the things a person must have, not what they want, would prefer or feel they deserve.

One of your most important responsibilities as a leader is to understand the wide range of needs of those around you. Understanding the needs of your staff will help you build morale, reach shared goals and lift performance. This is the key to understanding what makes people tick!

This deeper level of knowledge will enable a manager to maintain control when things go wrong. It will also improve their ability to meet goals, to better manage people and client relationships, to make better decisions, and to problem solve and innovate — all key assets for a high performance team.

Chapter summary

- Intuition can be learned. A fair proportion of intuition comes from the rational side of the brain, which is responsible for data analysis, rational and logical thinking—not gut feel.

- This style of thinking enables managers to anticipate and predict what is likely to happen in a range of situations.

- Empathy can be defined as 'an astute awareness of others' emotions, concerns and needs'. Our understanding of others' feelings and concerns flows from an awareness of our own.

- Empathy is an essential business skill as it is critical to persuasion and influence.

- Empathy drives *connection* between people, in turn driving the relationships required to sell what is created and innovated, be it a product or a concept.

- Don't confuse **empathy** with **sympathy**.

- Understanding others' needs without judging them is a critical skill in business. Those who don't will struggle to understand and work with others until they begin building skills in empathy.

- Empathy provides clues to what people want, need and value—essential components driving performance, creativity and innovation.

- Empathy helps to predict:
  - what people will do and how they will react in different situations
  - what their hot and cold buttons are
  - what brings out the worst and the very best in them.

- Those who are not open-minded or self-aware or who lack self-management skills will struggle to empathise with others.

- Successful organisations are those that work to understand what makes their people and their clients tick. An understanding of what people need distinguishes the top performers from the average.

Reflective questions

1. How intuitive would you say you are? What reasons would you give to validate?

2. How well do you pick up on what other people are thinking? Provide an example of how well you read a situation based on intuition.

3. How would you rate your empathy skills (scored out of 10)?

4. How would other people describe your empathy skills?

5. What would people say you are particularly good at?

6. What would they say you are not so good at?

7. How well do you understand the ethnic backgrounds of members of your team (scored out of 10)? Provide three examples of your understanding of their backgrounds.

8. How would you rate your listening skills?

9. How would your team rate your listening skills?

10. How sensitive would you say you are to other people's feelings?

11. Are you able to show empathy towards people you don't like? Provide an example.

12. How would you rate your level of control of your work? Does this affect your empathy skills? Discuss.

Where to start

1. In meetings make a mental note to listen twice as much as you speak and to ask more questions.

2. When someone is evidently unhappy, or is behaving inappropriately or out of character with you or in a situation, ask yourself why. What is it they fear? What need is not being met? What do they believe to be true?

3. Think about two people who have a great relationship, and identify the components at play that relate to empathy.

4. To test your Learned Intuition™ skills, sit down with someone you know well and watch a reality TV show in which people are being judged.

    (a) Compare your thoughts on what is really going on in different situations.

    (b) Try to predict and anticipate events.

    (c) Listen to the other person's point of view and compare them with your own.

chapter 6

How to connect people to the business

So far in the book we have looked at two key, behaviour-based manager mindsets that help build connection with others. They are to *be a role model*, connecting through trust, communication, inspiration and consistency of behaviour, and leading by example, and to *be empathetic*, understanding what makes people tick and how others see things.

Now we need to start to look at the things managers must *do*.

It has long been understood that one of the key skills required of a manager is to communicate effectively with their team. In today's business, however, this does not go far enough. Research shows that high-performing employees typically *feel connected*—and that typically it is high-performing managers who facilitate this connection.

So what is the difference between communication and connection? This is often not understood, so it can be helpful to think of them like this: At level 1 we communicate by sharing information with people or informing them. At level 2 we connect by ensuring people understand why something is important so they forge a level of *emotional connection to the message*. The act of connecting goes deeper than communication and takes more effort, time, skill and understanding of others to achieve.

Let's examine both levels in more detail.

Level 1: Communicate

Each year, businesses spend time, effort and money putting together complex strategies and business plans. This is done in the hope that business will grow, revenues will increase, and employee engagement and customer satisfaction will improve.

But what is often overlooked in the business plan is the need for regular review and deep scrutiny of communication methodologies that *are not* technology based! Of course communications technology is vitally important, but the place to make the biggest impact and achieve the biggest return is in analysing the *quality* of the communication between people inside the organisation and with clients outside the organisation.

In our experience most communication issues within organisations relate not to technology but to people. What this means is that most communication bottlenecks and misunderstandings will *not* be fixed by technology, as technology is merely a vehicle. Typical communication issues lie much deeper and are more often linked to lack of skill, lack of understanding and poor behavioural practices in people.

So where do you start when assessing the quality of the communication between people inside the organisation and clients outside the organisation?

Let's start by looking at the basics of business.

Most businesses are made up of products and/or services, people and processes. Communicating effectively across these three areas should be your number one priority, and only once you are achieving 90 per cent plus effectiveness in these areas should you move on to more complex strategies and more costly ideas; otherwise you will be wasting resources.

In reviewing communication across these three areas your goal must be to challenge and even discard your assumptions and identify the gap between intention, reality and perception. Once you are clear on this, your job as a manager is then to systematically close this gap by developing a strategy that then becomes an essential part of your business plan.

Your starting point, then, is to formulate questions that will test your assumptions about what is working and what is not in order to identify inefficiencies, error rates, loss of revenue and loss of opportunity.

Product communication

The key question here is, 'How competent are your people in communicating information about your product and company?' On a scale of 1 to 10, how would you score each member of your team on this question? What score would you give yourself? Our experience consistently shows a big gap between what managers think to be the case and what *is* the case.

Everyone within the organisation or team *must* be able to articulate clearly what you sell and what your company does. You may well be amazed how few people can do this — let alone do it well. What is even more amazing is how often sales or marketing people stumble over what it is they do or sell when talking to clients. They know it in their heads, but many cannot articulate and communicate it clearly.

As a manager, you must be confident that your people, especially those on the front line, can do this and you must drive the process hard. The good news is you have a great opportunity here to increase performance and profits. Test your assumptions against reality — you may be surprised!

People communication

To begin with, let's examine how effective people are in communicating information and knowledge between one another within the organisation. Your questions and analysis should test the *quality* of the communications.

Some typical assumptions that have the biggest impact on your business

'On the whole our managers are good communicators.'

The reality is that one in three managers admits that the hardest part of their job (and their weakest skill) is giving feedback, and yet this is *crucial* to raising performance.

'Our people seem to communicate effectively on email.'

When did you last look? The reality is that when managers were asked to review a random selection of emails sent by their staff, they were surprised and embarrassed by the poor quality of communication. Test this out. It's all about credibility; if credibility is lacking, connection will fail—and so will sales!

'On the whole, our sales people are good presenters.'

Our research indicated that salespeople typically found structuring a presentation and concentrating on the detail required to write and deliver it effectively *very* difficult. Keep in mind the skill set required to focus on detail. Structuring and drawing up an effective presentation requires a very different skill set from what salespeople are typically recruited for.

'Our written documentation is of a good standard.'

The reality is that most people in today's workforce were not taught how to write effectively at school, let alone in a professional business context.

'*We are fairly good at communicating between divisions.*'

In fact, this is rarely the case. Different divisions have different priorities. Cross-divisional communication is vitally important to both your team and the organisation in order to build loyalty and connection. People in other departments are more likely to deliver what you want, or to provide it faster, when they connect with you as a real person rather than just an email address. This is a common underlying issue for many teams we deal with and is very easily addressed.

Process communication

Your questions here should seek to test the quality of communication around the implementation of processes and procedures between people both within and outside of your organisation. These questions will help you to gauge how well things work and flow within your team or organisation.

- Do your current business issues relate to your people's understanding and application of processes and procedures?

- How competent are your people in applying the processes and procedures?

- Do they understand how what they do impacts the goal of the organisation?

- Do your people understand exactly how what they do affects those in other departments?

- How is process improvement encouraged?

- How is process improvement managed?

- How would you rate the quality and availability of procedural and process manuals and other documentation?

The final step in evaluating your communication practices is to consider wastage across these areas.

The following questions identify the four areas where most waste occurs in relation to what we have discussed in this chapter.

- How much time, money and effort is wasted on client visits by salespeople who cannot clearly articulate the basics?

- How much time, money and effort is wasted on written information that clients and staff don't understand or don't want to read?

- How much time, money and effort is wasted on process manuals and procedures that are rarely referred to?

- How much time, money and effort is wasted on emails that are not read or actioned?

So far we have focused on communication. Now we need to move up to the next level.

Level 2: Connect

Connection is the process of ensuring people understand why something is important, so they forge a level of *emotional connection to the message*.

Once your people understand and can articulate what you do, the next step is to help them understand more about convincing and persuading others through emotion. This is typically achieved by explaining the 'why'. Understanding why compels people to act. Teaching people about the why is extremely important, because simply telling people to do things no longer works in business today.

First, people need to know why we should do things a certain way and what the ramifications are, in terms of impact on other people, processes and the company, if they are not done as required. This information will connect your people to the importance of doing things a certain way. It will also provoke an emotion in them if they choose not to do it in this way. Depending on the person, this emotion might be guilt, insecurity or fear of potential conflict, for example.

Second, people also need to connect to how working with this company fits with who they are as people, in terms of their needs, values and beliefs. This connects people to their personal why, which is very powerful. The emotions evoked here — for example, pride, satisfaction, happiness and optimism — are more positive.

More and more people understand the concept of 'start with why', an idea introduced by Simon Sinek in his book of the same name. However, where people and organisations go wrong is that they try to complete this task during induction. This approach can be problematic, though, as people first need to fully understand what the organisation does and how they fit in it; only then can they fully connect to the why.

So, although induction is good place to start, connection usually fails here, as people are so bombarded with information that they struggle to process it all. Instead, encourage them to start by coming to grips with what you do, and then continue to work on connection to the why throughout *all* stages of employment.

Many people we have worked with have revealed that they only 'got' the why a few years after joining the organisation but when they did, they got a flash of inspiration fuelling a stronger connection to the business.

As manager, connecting your people to the why effectively requires a depth of knowledge and understanding about *each of your people.* You need to provide them with the context of why the organisation is doing what it is doing. Once this is understood by them, work to help them find their why and connect it to the business.

To take one example, let's look at a job most people would not want to do — garbage collection. As a manager, how would you connect a person to a garbage collection organisation? The key here is to challenge your assumptions and preconceived ideas, because for some it is a great job!

If you were to ask garbage collectors why they do the job they do, their reasons might include that the hours are great and mean they have time for their family; that it gives them a daily 'gym' workout, which they get paid for; that it gives them free time during the day to study or pursue other interests; that they are passionate about the environment; or that as a second job it helps with family expenses or savings.

Once you understand such reasons, then connecting people to your organisation should become a little easier.

So the why comes only with an understanding of what makes a person tick. Then that person's why should be matched to the why of the organisation to strengthen the connection to the business. It is a process that must be handled carefully and respectfully or there is a risk of an outcome that is the complete opposite of what is intended — that is, *disconnection*.

I have seen the following example play out many times.

A line manager hears that David on his team is expecting to be a father. The line manager already knows David and his wife are saving for a house, and he assumes that David will now be more motivated and interested in how to achieve a higher bonus and make more money.

So the next time the manager catches up with David he gets out the calculator and starts to do the numbers on how to achieve a 10 per cent growth in the next quarter, and what that then translates into in bonus potential for David. But during the meeting David shows no interest whatsoever. For some reason, which the manager is unable to pinpoint, the whole message seems to have been lost on him.

What went wrong?

The manager attempted to connect David to his bonus potential as a way to inspire and motivate him. The big problem here is that David's why is related to the people he works with. He is not driven by money. The manager missed the mark — as so many do — and disrespected David in the process by implying he probably needed more money because of his circumstances.

Finally, remember that a person's why may also change over time. Your why in your twenties will be very different from your why in your thirties, forties, fifties and beyond.

We also need to understand that for many people there is no why beyond making ends meet. In fact, most people we've interviewed, no matter what their income or job, have yet to discover their why. They may have thought about it, but for many this seemingly higher, 'nobler' purpose eludes them. Their why right now is doing their job to support themselves and their family, until such time as they identify their purpose and can go after it — and there is nothing wrong with that.

Chapter summary

- *Communicate and inform* through sharing information with people.

- *Connect* to ensure people understand why something is important, so they can forge a level of emotional connection to the message.

- For the biggest impact and return, analyse the quality of the communication between people both within and outside the organisation.

- A manager should avoid making assumptions and identify the gaps between intention, reality and perception.

- Everyone within the team must be able to clearly articulate what your organisation sells and/or does.

- A manager provides context on why the organisation is doing what it is doing. Once this is understood by the team, work to help them find their why to make a connection.

- Understanding the why will connect your people to the importance of doing things a certain way.

- Communication is of vital importance to both your team and the organisation in order to build loyalty and connection.

- People in other departments are more likely to deliver more of what you want or provide it faster once they perceive you as a real person and not just an email address.

- When considering the people, products and processes of an organisation, there should also be a focus on any wastage that may be occurring.

- An employee's why may change over time. Their why in their twenties could be very different from their why in their thirties, forties, fifties and beyond.

Reflective questions

1. How competent are my people in communicating information about our product and company?

2. Do you communicate clearly how your product or service meets people's needs?

3. Do you communicate clearly how your product or service is better than your competitors'?

4. How competent are my people in applying processes and procedures?

5. Do my people understand how what it is they do impacts the goal of the organisation?

6. Do my people understand how what they do impacts people in other departments?

7. How is process improvement encouraged?

8. What is the quality and availability of procedural and process manuals?

9. Do you know if your sales people are able to clearly articulate what it is you sell and offer?

10. Do you produce written information that clients and staff don't understand or don't want to read?

Where to start

1. **Communicate (people).** Ensure your team is fully informed about the company, their role and what is expected of them. Do they need updating or clarification?

2. **Communicate (process).** Ensure your procedural and process manuals are current. Do they need updating or clarification?

3. **Connect with clients/customers.** Help your team understand the difference between communication and connection, and the importance of establishing a connection with clients/customers. The better they are at doing this the more they will be able to convince and persuade others.

4. **Find the why.** Work to connect each person in your team to the organisational why and then help them to define or build on their personal why.

chapter 7

How to create a personal connection

It starts and ends with YOU!

A core component of the connection mindset is to look very carefully at how you *personally connect* with people. This is important, as the degree to which you personally connect with others will determine their level of interest in you, what they say to you and do for you, their perception of you and their loyalty to you (how far they will go for you).

One area to explore is the impact of your personal 'presence'.

Presence is a tricky concept to understand. Like the X factor, it's hard to describe and define, just something you feel or sense about someone. When you ask people what presence means to them, the typical descriptions include charisma and rapport; someone has a sort of 'aura' about them. Most people think it is a natural attribute and you either have it or you don't. It is not something you work on, it's just there when they walk into a room.

It is important to understand that to have presence is not always a positive thing. We can all relate to the idea that when certain individuals walk into a room they immediately lift the atmosphere in a positive way. But equally there are those in whose presence the general mood sinks, and then there are those whose entry goes virtually unnoticed. So presence generates a feeling and this feeling can make people feel either up or down or merely indifferent.

This response is important for managers to understand, as their presence will have a direct impact on the work environment and affect productivity levels by motivating or demotivating people.

The line manager looking for better results and higher performance should aim to radiate a presence that will lift people and inspire them to perform. You do not want to be the person who walks into a room with zero response or, worse still, to see the mood of the team instantly deflate. If this is what you see, it means your presence alone is creating feelings of unease, threat or insecurity. The best managers understand the direct impact their presence can have on productivity levels and work hard to foster a feeling of safety rather than threat.

A common problem here is that the managers who do fuel the feelings of threat and danger in their team are unaware of it or don't accept that it is happening. This usually boils down to low self-awareness or poor self-control.

We have discussed self-awareness and self-control, and you will already have some clues on how to improve skills and behaviours in these areas. The next step is to look at others' perception of you in terms of your personal presence and impact at work.

Although most consider presence as part of an unconscious mindset, conversations we have had with managers who have it suggest they do know what they are doing and are being more purposeful than others might think. Typically, they are adopting a particular mindset, and in exploring this mindset we will find the clues we need to understand how to develop it in ourselves.

So where do we start?

First, what does it take to forge a positive impression in the mind of another? Let's start with the basics. We know that we communicate messages to others through three main channels: our body language, our voice (tone) and our words.

When we consider that 70 per cent of information is communicated through body language, 23 per cent via tone and only 7 per cent via words, we start to get the picture of where we need to concentrate our efforts!

Other research tells us the core elements that make the biggest impact—either positive or negative—are personal presentation, body language, tone, spoken word, written word and social presence.

Personal presentation

If you are a leader with 'executive presence', suggests Sylvia Ann Hewlett in her book of the same name, you manifest:

> an amalgam of qualities that telegraphs that you are in charge or deserve to be ... no one ever bothers to assess your communication skills or your leadership capabilities if your appearance telegraphs that you are clueless.

There is no doubt that first impressions count, and the very first thing people notice when you walk into a room is what you are wearing and how you put yourself forward. Although some people are uncomfortable with this 'judgemental' mindset, you need to assess how important it is to you and your job that you create a positive impression through how you dress and present yourself.

For most of us, even if we disagree with it in principle, it is very important. The fact is, if you want to be taken seriously at work and with clients, you need to look the part.

In recent years, a range of different dress codes have come into play in organisations, but the most popular one is still 'business'. And with this comes common themes and expectations.

We asked recruiters and senior managers the following questions:

1. What impact does someone's personal appearance have on you?

2. What aspects of personal appearance stand out most for you?

3. How does this influence your judgement of how a person operates at work or does business?

4. What in this context is considered unprofessional?

The five most common factors influencing perception, it turns out, are personal hygiene, clean and groomed hair and nails, well-presented (clean, ironed) clothes that fit well and are not too revealing, and clean and well-kept shoes (especially the heels for women).

How you as a manager look *every* day is important. You are a role model and should be consistent in the signals you give out. You need to show that you care about your appearance and take pride in yourself. Dressing professionally demonstrates self-respect and respect for those around you.

Remember, if you break the rules, you are giving your staff 'permission' to do the same. It really does all come down to setting an example. Also bear in mind that how a person presents themselves has a significant impact on their mood and confidence levels. People who dress well tend to feel the part, become more confident and feel better about themselves, feelings that then radiate to form positive impressions among others.

Body language
As indicated above, your body language is a highly significant communication channel, conveying your mood and attitude. A person comes into work in the morning and within

seconds everyone in the team knows if that person is in a good or bad mood.

As a manager, how you present yourself, from the time you get to work to the moment you leave, has an impact on everyone. People are feeding off your signals and, consciously or subconsciously, making decisions about how they will or will not interact with you. More importantly, they are deciding whether they will tell you what you need to know or what they think you want to hear!

If your body language discourages people from approaching you or communicating with you honestly, this will cause problems for everyone. Your body language includes your facial expressions, posture and gestures.

Typically, your facial expressions reveal your mood and demeanour. They have a great impact on how people feel in your presence, and that influences how they think and operate.

Think about how you *look at* people. You need to be aware of what impression people have of your expressions and how that makes them feel. If they feel any kind of discomfort or safety threat, you will not be able to communicate effectively with them.

Your goal should be to encourage people to be genuine, sincere and forthright with you, which means you need to make others feel safe and comfortable in your presence.

Make sure to get feedback from those closest to you to find out what other people might think but perhaps not share with you.

It is important that you understand what you *don't mean* to imply through your body language. I have met senior people whose body language intimidates people, yet they had no clue to what degree it was happening. The smallest things they did made the biggest impact — even something as simple as how they sit in a meeting or how they cross their legs!

Think about the 'resting style' of your face. How would you describe your face when it is expressionless? Take a photo and look at what mood it suggests. Is it smiley, serious, angry, vacant, sad, detached?

A very funny video released in 2013 by Taylor Orci describes the 'bitchy resting face' phenomenon, a term that has now caught on in pop culture via online videos and social media. In a nutshell, it talks about the negative impact an unintentionally severe expression can have on others. Those who have a more serious resting face are commonly judged to be aloof, intimidating, judgemental, unfriendly, uninterested, snobbish or simply unimpressed.

Remember, lighter people draw people in. More serious people push people away as they appear to threaten their safety. Which are you? Look in the mirror!

One way to gauge your resting face is through the questions or comments you find yourself fielding. If people ask you what's wrong or if you are okay, you may have a serious resting face. Similarly, if friends say you are not the person they thought you were when they first met you, and how they thought you were aloof or unfriendly, you may have cause for concern.

So if you think you have a naturally serious face, you need to compensate for it in other ways—for example, by making other aspects of your body language warmer, smiling more, lightening your tone of voice and using more open gestures.

Tone

As already noted, your tone of voice accounts for 23 per cent of your communication and often will mean the difference between connecting with another person or not. Think about when you listen to people on the radio. You can't help but form opinions of them by the way they speak—not so much their accent (although that may be a factor) but by their voice and intonation, how fast or slow they speak and so on. For some, regardless of the words they use and whether they look the part, if the tone is not right, connection fails.

Think about a voice on the radio or television that turns you off. You literally switch channels when you hear it. As a manager, you must think carefully about your tone and voice and what they may imply. The last thing you want is for your people to tune out on you!

Ask yourself and those around you these questions:

- Does your tone lift people up and keep them interested?

- Does your tone indicate you are interested in the views of others?

- Does your tone vary in pitch or is it closer to a monotone?

- Does your tone make others feel safe or unsafe?

- Is your tone respectful and caring?

- Is your tone unintentionally harsh or condescending?

- Do you speak too fast or too slow?

- Do you speak too softly or too loudly?

Pay attention to these traits in yourself in meetings, and reflect on your tone and its impact on others. Remember, if you give bad tone you will get bad tone! More often than not your tone will be reflected or mirrored back to you.

Spoken word

What you say is a result of what you think. Therefore what comes out of your mouth represents the type of person you are and how you approach life. In *1984*, George Orwell suggested that 'if thought corrupts language, language can also corrupt thought'.

Does your language signify a 'glass half full' or 'glass half empty' personality? Does your language signify you are polite and well mannered? Is your language bossy, blunt, friendly, long winded, professional or informal? All this paints a picture and will influence how you interact, connect with or disconnect from others.

Your family will be able to help you here. Typically, how you talk at home indicates how you talk at work, as your language, personality and thinking patterns are unlikely to change dramatically between the two environments.

Think about (and seek out feedback on) the kind of language you use. Do you speak in a straightforward way or do people tend to ask you to clarify a lot? Do you tend to speak formally, politely, casually?

Written word

Another key communication channel is the written word. This plays a major role in creating the impression others form of you. Your written 'presence' is as important as your personal presence, especially for those who interact with people mainly via written correspondence, rather than face to face or by phone.

This is an area where people gain an impression of you and draw conclusions relating to how they perceive your level of education or class, how you do business, what type of person you are, and whether or not you 'care'. As this list implies, the judgements can be quite harsh, totally subjective and unfounded. As a manager you must ensure your written word accurately represents you and is of a high standard.

The good news is that business writing has become simplified over the years. There is no more need for flowery language. Today people just want to understand what you are saying as quickly as possible. The guidelines for business writing now focus on clarity, simplicity and courtesy.

While each organisation may have its own 'house style guide' for written communications, the following 10 rules are the most common in current use.

The 10 rules to modern business writing

1. Write to express, not to impress. Avoid fancy words that make you look smart—just focus on getting your message across clearly.

2. Write for your reader! It's about them, not you, so adapt *your* style to suit *theirs*.

3. Take a 'personal approach'. This means using people's and organisations' names and personal pronouns such as 'you', 'me', 'I' and 'we' wherever appropriate and not resorting to the third person ('We would like...' rather than 'The organisation would like...'; 'I would appreciate...' rather than 'It would be appreciated...').

4. When writing, your aim should be to encourage your reader to *want* to read your document, to *understand* your message and to *take the action* you require them to!

5. Where possible, use short, simple words and avoid jargon ('mission critical', 'interface') and acronyms (people may not understand them).

6. Use short sentences (no more than 12 to 15 words, where possible) and bullet points wherever possible. Avoid wordy phrases ('September' rather than 'in the month of September').

7. Use short paragraphs of four to seven lines (no more than 100 words). Each paragraph should contain one main idea or point only. Begin each paragraph with a sentence that explains the main point of the paragraph. For technical documents, aim for an average paragraph length of 40 words or three to four lines.

(continued)

The 10 rules to modern business writing (cont'd)

8. To guide your reader, use 'linking words' to show the connections between your paragraphs ('Next', 'Similarly', 'As a result').

9. Maintain standards. Your professional standards give the reader certain perceptions about you and your company. Always proofread your documents and ensure your formatting is correct. Poor spelling and formatting will prompt your readers to disconnect.

10. Spell their name right. There will be instant disconnection if you don't!

Social presence

The extraordinary rise of social media should convince us that the ability to communicate and connect with people informally is of utmost importance to our teams.

In our view, social media is an excellent way to inspire, communicate, share, teach and mentor your team. It should be used to reinforce messages, to allow people to get to know you better, to express ideas and points of view, and, of course, to build bonds and deeper connections with and among your people.

For some managers a mindset shift is required. There is a fine line between connecting at work and connecting work to your personal life. You must think this through carefully and evaluate how you can bridge the two in a way that is comfortable for you and your team.

My advice is to find a way, as the use of social media to engage with your team can be fun and is great for building strong connections. For those who prefer to connect with their teams solely in a traditional work context, I would encourage you to be more lighthearted in your approach and show a less formal side to yourself, as this is what will strengthen connections with your people.

Let's look at some of the current social media options available:

- One of the fastest growing media platforms is Pinterest, which is a sort of online scrapbook. Here, you can collect your favourite images and pin them to themed boards. You and your team could collect and share pictures of common interests, create team dream boards, and share motivational quotes and book recommendations. This is a great tool for getting to know one another better, sharing common interests—and even learning and reinforcing messages.

- Another popular social networking platform, the micro-blogging site Tumblr, is a great place to share ideas, interests, pictures and much more.

- You could set up a private Facebook group for your team, where they can share ideas, thoughts, news, opinions and pictures, and this could be then linked to the mobile sharing service Instagram. WhatsApp is another great application you can use to set up a private group to share news, comments and photos with your team.

- Twitter is great for those managers or leaders who want to connect to larger teams more frequently than they are currently able to do. It's a time-effective way to share what inspires you, what makes you tick and your vision for the organisation. This can also be a great tool for reinforcing cultural change, values-based messages and new product updates.

- Another option is to use one of these social networking platforms to start a virtual book club. Here you can choose a book, set time frames for reading chapters, then get people to use Facebook, Twitter or Tumblr to comment on the ideas and what they have learned. It provides a different way to communicate with your team, share ideas, learn—and connect.

Chapter summary

■ Work to ensure your presence lifts the mood of a room and motivates people.

■ Communication is a combination of body language, tone and words—use all three effectively.

■ Your personal appearance and 'resting face' influence the people around you. Use them to demonstrate respect for yourself and others.

■ Your tone of voice and choice of words reflect your professionalism. Use them wisely.

■ When writing, keep it clear, simple and courteous.

■ How you as a manager look every day is important. You are a role model and you need to be consistent in the signals you convey.

■ Your goal should be to encourage people to be genuine, sincere and forthright with you. To achieve this, you need to make others feel 'safe' with you.

■ If you have a naturally serious face, compensate by smiling more, lightening your tone of voice and using more open gestures.

■ Your choice of words indicates the type of person you are and how you approach life.

■ Write for your reader. It's about them, not you! Adapt *your* style to suit *theirs*.

Reflective questions

1. How would you describe your personal presence currently?

2. Do you walk into a room and lift the mood? How do you know?

3. Do people generally feel positive around you?

4. How much effort do you put into your appearance (on a scale of 1–10)?

5. How would you rate your levels of personal hygiene (on a scale of 1–10)?

6. Which areas of your personal presentation could be improved?

7. Describe the 'resting style' of your face.

8. Describe how you walk.

9. What gestures do you use?

10. How well mannered are you? Provide five examples.

11. How would people describe your tone of voice on most days?

Where to start

1. Ask your friends what their impression of you was when they first met you.

2. Video yourself giving a presentation and critique it:

    (a) Do you look professional?

    (b) What style of language do you use?

    (c) Describe your tone.

    (d) Describe your body language.

3. Select a social media channel for you and your team to use and communicate with them on areas related to work and personal aspects of their lives.

4. Assess your level of connection with each member of your team and decide on strategies for how to better connect and interact with them.

5. Test your document's readability scores according to the Flesch Reading Ease test. Visit www.fourmindsets.com to find out more.

chapter 8

How to have a challenging conversation without breaking connection

Previous chapters have discussed the importance of communicating and connecting in business and the impact your personal presence has on this. In this chapter we'll examine how to focus those skills on the area that nearly every manager we speak to says is the hardest to master — the challenging conversation.

Research and feedback indicates that the main concern managers have about this type of conversation is that, if not handled correctly, it has the potential to break a strong connection in a moment. As a result, managers will typically postpone or avoid having the conversation altogether. If they do initiate the conversation, they usually fail to adequately plan how to manage it or ensure they are in the right mindset for it.

A challenging conversation is one where there is a high likelihood that opinions between the participants will differ and as a result emotions will be triggered.

The following model was developed to help a manager cover all the steps needed for a challenging conversation to achieve a successful outcome, positively impact the mindset of the other person—and maintain connection.

The TALKING Process model is designed to help the manager to:

- plan and execute a challenging conversation

- build rapport and reinforce mutual respect

- reinforce mutual purpose

- ensure the conversation is as objective as possible

- reveal and test assumptions and perceptions.

Step 1: Timing and preparation

A key element of handling a challenging conversation successfully is understanding the appropriate timing.

It is important to choose the right time for the conversation. Leaving it too late can be seen as avoidance, and with this comes the loss of impact and relevance to the situation in hand. On the other hand, having the conversation too soon also has its problems. You need to consider whether it is a one-off situation or if it indicates a trend occurring that needs to be addressed.

The timing also needs to account for allowing yourself enough time to prepare. All too often, a challenging conversation becomes far more difficult than it needs to be because the manager failed to prepare. Typically, the 80:20 rule should be applied—that is, 80 per cent of time spent on preparation and 20 per cent on the conversation itself.

The easiest way to keep a conversation timely and on track is to consider its actual purpose. What exactly is the problem and how can you articulate it? Sometimes core problems can become entangled in other issues, so it is important you are clear on what the core issues are so the conversation does not become sidetracked.

A key element to preparation is to think about and anticipate the likely responses of the other person. Planning for their responses in advance will save you time and help you to plan to control your emotions.

This stage requires careful consideration and planning, as it often makes the difference between success and failure. The reality is that people rarely surprise us and we know how they are likely to respond in various situations. In planning your conversation, consider what past experience has taught you about this person's personality. What are their emotional triggers, and how do they demonstrate their emotions?

Next, consider their likely responses and decide what would be the best approach to dealing with them. For example, if they shut down, what will you say? If they overreact, how will you deal with it? If they push your buttons, how will you maintain control?

Finally, perhaps the most important part of getting into the right mindset for having this conversation is to objectively consider what was or is your part in the problem. How have you contributed to the situation—positively or negatively? What should you take responsibility for?

Once you have considered these questions, you might find your mindset changes and perhaps even that the need to have the conversation disappears.

For example, perhaps the initial objective of the conversation was to discuss why the person is not meeting their key performance indicators. But thinking through this in more detail, you realise you have never had a conversation with this person to review these goals since they went through their induction.

Step 2: Ask questions

One of a manager's key skills is asking the right questions to define and isolate an issue and find a resolution to it. Asking appropriate questions when handling challenging conversations will help solve any problems efficiently and effectively. Managers should have a bank of questions prepared for every conversation they have. Part of the planning process *must* be considering the questions you will ask. In each case, think about what you need to find out and qualify or verify *before* you start to speak!

A common mistake is for a manager to go into an interaction with their own reasoning already laid out. Their intention is to talk and to sell their own ideas and views, rather than to ask questions and validate perceptions and assumptions. As a result, they miss out on excellent opportunities to improve the quality of their conversations, show they are interested in hearing the other person's point of view, and discover information that could aid a resolution, save time and inspire new ideas—all essential to high performance in business. Remember Stephen Covey's advice: 'Seek first to understand.'

During your preparation, consider what are the relevant questions you should be asking. To help yourself decide, put yourself into a mindset where you no longer assume that you already know what the problem is and that you have the solution. While asking questions and objectively exploring the other person's point of view, you should be prepared to change your viewpoint.

Once you have done this, you need to choose the style of questions most relevant to demonstrating and maintaining this mindset. If the other person feels that you already have your answer and are merely going through the motions, your 'connection' will break.

To help you prepare your questions, consider the different types of questions:

Open questions start with words such as *how, would, what* or *which*. Their purpose is to encourage a conversational response rather than a simple yes or no.

'Would you tell me how you are planning to present your findings?'

'What are some of the challenges you are facing this quarter?'

Closed questions often start with words such as *have, do, did, can, will, could, are.* Their purpose is either to elicit a short, often one-word answer or to confirm facts.

'Do you have authority to sign off?'

'When did your client receive the product?'

Probing questions tend to start with phrases such as *Tell me more, You mentioned, What happened then?* Their purpose is often to follow on from an open or closed question to gather more detail on a particular piece of information provided.

'You mentioned that...'

'Tell me more about how you plan to...'

Leading/assumptive questions start with words such as *Presumably, I assume that, I take it that.* Their purpose is to facilitate agreement in order to arrive at a solution.

'I would imagine that...'

'I take it that you are happy with...'

'I assume that you will now...'

Also keep in mind the way you ask questions, including your tone of voice and ensuring the other person doesn't feel like you are 'setting them up' with your questions.

'What time do we start work in the morning?'

Although this is a good example of a closed question, there is potential for the person to feel threatened or set up. If they say they don't know, they will feel foolish; and if they say 8.30, they may feel threatened.

'Why did you complete the process that way?'

Again, this could be interpreted as threatening. Asking a lot of 'why' questions may be perceived as challenging and will risk breaking your connection. A better approach might be 'Tell me how you completed the project'.

Step 3: Listen, look and learn tips

Once you have your prepared questions, it is then time to ensure you are in the right mindset to listen for the answers, look for reactions, emotions or safety threats, and maintain an open mind. Using this approach, you will be able to learn something new about the situation or to confirm your perceptions were indeed correct.

It is also important to note that managing a challenging conversation requires two styles of listening: *precision listening* and *empathetic listening*.

When precision listening the objective is to listen for the facts and detail of the other person's communication. When empathetic or empathic listening (also called active or reflective listening), on the other hand, listen for the emotional content behind the words.

Several skills are required of a good listener. These important skills will persuade the person either that they are indeed being heard or, conversely, that you are not listening to or 'hearing' them. People who perceive (correctly or incorrectly) that they are not being heard will typically feel that you are not interested in their concerns, that you don't respect or value them.

All of which will potentially contribute to an escalation of the situation and break connection.

So, to demonstrate you are listening, here are some tips to send the right messages to the other person.

Tip 1: Paraphrase

As listener, repeat (in your own words) what you understand the speaker has said. Paraphrasing enables the listener to check that they have picked up on (a) what has been said and (b) what is not being said (that is, the speaker's feelings).

'What I am hearing you say is that you ...'

Some tips for paraphrasing:

- Pay careful attention to the speaker's basic message, which includes looking out for (a) non-verbal messages, (b) tone of voice and (c) how the speaker is feeling.

- Use your own words when paraphrasing what has been said; don't quote verbatim.

After paraphrasing, look for some cue or sign from the other person that indicates whether your statement was accurate, or ask the speaker directly.

Tip 2: Clarify and confirm

By clarifying a point, you ensure that you correctly understand the situation and show the speaker you are 'with them' and listening carefully.

Remember, people want to be 'heard' and can become upset or agitated when this does not happen. So this is a great way to show you are truly listening.

> 'You mentioned that the client received the product at 9am yesterday—is that right?'

Some tips for when you clarify and confirm:

- Never assume you know what the person means.

- In practice, words mean what each person thinks they mean.

- Words describe thoughts and experiences, which are unique to each of us.

- Clarification of meaning leads to shared understanding.

  > 'I would like you to clarify a point...'

  > 'Do you mean...'

  > 'Can we explore that point further...'

  > 'So what you are saying is...'

  > 'So what I am hearing is...'

Remember, you have two ears and one mouth—so use them proportionally!

Step 4: Knowledge sharing

Only at this point in a conversation should you share your thoughts, ideas, point of view and knowledge.

We have spent a good deal of time looking at how to connect with people. It is at this point that you need to put these principles into practice as you share knowledge or information that may make the other person uncomfortable, insecure or fearful. If they feel this way, they are unlikely to 'hear' exactly what you are saying, so the message may be lost.

Your delivery is therefore vitally important. Concentrate on dealing with any fear and anxiety and putting the other person at ease. Your objective should be to have a conversation with minimum emotion, as emotion clouds judgement and possible outcomes.

Remember, your body language, your tone of voice, the words you use and even how you are sitting will impact their thoughts and mindset.

At this point in the conversation you will have tested your theories about the issue behind the conversation by asking appropriate questions. The next step is to put forward your point of view clearly, succinctly and fairly.

This is the final part of the assumption testing process. At this point, you are laying out your version of what is happening or has happened. Remember, there is no judgement at this point. You just want the other person to hear how you see things and to learn if there is still anything you are unaware of.

It is important to remember that we often tell ourselves 'stories' that help us to confirm and qualify our own position — regardless of whether they are real or relevant. These stories are based on what we *think* to be the truth.

It is critical that at this stage you talk only about what you *know* to be true. This way, you also ensure that your potential feelings and thoughts about the other person are set aside and that you are dealing only with objective data.

'Thank you for sharing that information with me ...'

'I would like to now just take the time to explain to you ...'

'I hear what you are saying and would like to let you know ...'

These examples are non-threatening and clear. You have listened to them and it is only fair that they now listen to your take on things.

> ## Knowledge sharing checklist
>
> ✓ Share what you know—not what you think.
>
> ✓ Concentrate on maintaining connection: try to understand how they see things, even if you don't agree.
>
> ✓ Check your body language, words and tone of voice.

Step 5: Identify issues

During the first four stages, you maintain an open frame of mind. Through listening, asking questions and sharing what you know, your objective has been to clarify the situation through testing and confirming the underlying information.

At this point you need to be clear on what underlying issues have been revealed and to discuss them. The aim is to ensure you both understand the key issues. From this point, you are now starting to 'close' the conversation.

It is possible that you will find out there is something else you did not know or that the other person feels your account of the issues does not match theirs. However, given the emphasis on a factual review of the issues, there should not be much room for disagreement.

> 'So, given I was [you were] unaware that... this is how I see it... The issue we are now dealing with is ...'

Your aim during each of these stages is to gain mutual agreement. There will be situations where the other person will continue to disagree. Remember, though, that you have given every opportunity to the other person to be heard, to share and to provide information. Finally you, as manager, may need to drive the close of the conversation to avoid a circular repetition of arguments or diversions.

Step 6: Needs

Once you have confirmed the core issues (agreed or not), you must be able to explain *why* these issues are important and who the issues affect.

During a challenging conversation, the core issues raised will affect the organisation in some way. This may be because the needs of an individual, a team, a manager (including you) are not being met or because of an issue with organisational policies, procedures, rules or standards.

Once you have identified the core issue, you then need to explain *how* this impacts the organisation. (If it doesn't, then the issue becomes one of a personal nature.)

Your job is to explain which needs have not been met and consequently what needs to be done or achieved now and why.

Only when people understand can they change. Only by describing the needs of the organisation and what the impact will be is there any chance of a change in behaviour. In many cases, referring to rules or regulations is not enough to convince or compel the other person to make a change or to get something done. Often you will have to 'sell' the need for a change by describing the reason, relevance or what will be achieved.

The purpose of this stage is to convince the other person of the importance of taking the action and what the possible ramifications could be if this is not done.

Needs checklist

✓ Needs explain why the issues are important.

✓ Needs must be identified to convince the other person that the issues are important.

✓ Identify the needs and requirements in terms of the organisation, the team and you.

✓ Your role in this step is to sell the reason, the relevance and the why.

✓ Selling the link to why it's important is essential to change behaviour.

✓ Needs identify why the conversation is important.

✓ Needs identify the ramifications of what could happen if a particular action is not taken.

Step 7: Gain commitment

This is the most important part of the process. Without this step, it is unlikely that anything will be achieved.

It is quite often the case that people are so happy to have got through the conversation that they forget to allocate accountabilities and responsibilities for the next steps. This step tells both parties what has been achieved and what happens from here.

It also reinforces the importance of the conversation and the process you have both just been through, thus serving to formalise the proceedings.

Gain commitment checklist

✓ Agree to a plan and gain commitment.

✓ Agree on actions.

✓ Agree on responsibilities.

✓ Agree on time frames and checkpoints.

✓ Always follow up in writing.

Chapter summary

- Timing for the conversation is very important. Put it off for too long and you may be accused of avoidance. Hold it too soon and you may have insufficient understanding of its potential.

- Prepare and plan the conversation using the 80:20 rule.

- Don't assume you already know the answer or what the issue is. Ensure you ask appropriate and relevant questions to test your assumptions.

- Listen to facts (through precision listening) and pay attention to what feelings are being demonstrated (through empathetic listening).

- Look out for visual signs and verbal cues for any underlying issues of the other party.

- Identify your 'needs' and understand their 'needs'.

- Create and maintain empathy and work to build rapport with the other party.

- Don't be distracted by points that are irrelevant to the conversation or be caught up with emotion. Acknowledge that there are strong feelings about the situation but stay focused on what needs to be achieved.

- Convince the other party as to why finding and agreeing to a solution is important.

- Once you've come to an agreement, use the momentum to put a plan of action in place and gain commitment to it from the other party there and then.

Reflective questions

1. Think about the last challenging conversation you had. How much time — how many minutes or hours — did you spend preparing for it?

2. On reflection, did the person behave any differently from how you would have expected, or was their behaviour fairly typical of them?

3. Why did the conversation become challenging for you?

4. If you were to ask a close friend or family member how they know when you are stressed, what would they say? Do you think you show this to your team too?

5. What was your part in the problem being discussed? What could you have done to prevent the problem increasing?

6. What questions did you ask during the conversation?

7. Provide examples of how you actually showed you were listening carefully to the other person. What techniques did you use?

8. If you were to be really honest how open-minded were you on entering the conversation (on a scale of 1–10)?

9. At the end of the conversation was there absolute clarity on what the next steps were and when they were to be achieved by? Provide an example.

10. On reflection, what will you do differently next time?

Where to start

1. Before your next conversation, promise yourself you will print off the checklist at www.fourmindsets.com to help you quickly prepare.

2. Ask someone close to you to give you feedback on how people would perceive you in a challenging conversation. What signals do you give off?

3. With every challenging conversation you have from here, identify the potentially tricky areas beforehand: which of your buttons could be pushed? Now prepare yourself ahead of time so as to avoid the potential flashpoints and put your best foot forward.

4. Always, always, always ask yourself: what part did I play in this issue? What did I potentially do or not do that has contributed to the situation?

Part III

The Growth Mindset

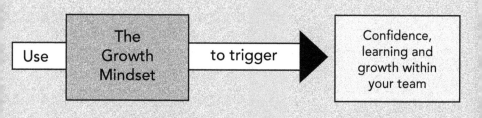

Use | The Growth Mindset | to trigger | Confidence, learning and growth within your team

In this Part:

➤ How to teach people confidence

➤ The manager as trainer—how to share knowledge and train your team quickly

➤ How learners think and how to adapt your style

➤ The manager as coach and mentor—10 essential tips

chapter 9

How to teach people confidence

One of the most important and significant roles of a manager is to help your people gain confidence in their roles. Confidence is essential for all high-performing individuals and teams. Building confidence in your team members ensures they keep growing, stretching their abilities and attaining new skills they often did not know they were even capable of.

Our experience shows that the best managers see qualities in individuals that the individual themselves sometimes cannot see. These managers identify hidden potential and actively work towards building confidence in that person to help them realise it.

We have worked with numerous people in whom we have recognised potential, actively boosting their confidence using a structured process, until at some point they could see it themselves and feel confident enough to go after it themselves.

Think about it: how do *you* help build your team's confidence levels? Contrary to what many people think, confidence *is* a teachable skill that a person is not necessarily born with.

There is a specific pathway to building people's confidence, and as a manager you should know it and develop it in others every day. But first you must understand that there are two types of confidence, *confident competence* and *confident incompetence.*

There is a strong correlation between competence and confidence; that is, the more *competent* you are, the more *confident* you become. However, the reverse is *not* true: becoming more confident does *not* mean you become more competent.

To be clear, confident competence is derived from true competence. Confident incompetence, on the other hand, is derived from a *perception* of personal competence that does not exist. Think of TV shows such as *American Idol* and you get the picture. Many of these people genuinely believe they can sing when they show up in front of the judges! As a manager, you must build a team based on *confident competence.* So how do you do this?

First you must understand that a lack of confidence usually comes from a lack of aptitude or awareness of some sort. In some cases, it can derive from deep-rooted situations or emotional issues, but in the main this is not the case, and this is not our focus in this book. Our interest is in identifying what aptitude or awareness is missing and what knowledge is needed to fill the gap.

You should be aware that any lack of awareness, aptitude or knowledge generally shows up in individuals as some form of fear or insecurity. This is usually manifested in negative behaviour such as avoidance or aggression or overcompensating behaviour such as talking up a situation or boasting.

So when this happens, instead of getting irritated or judgemental or taking things personally, as many managers do, ask yourself what it may be that they are insecure about or fearful of—what could be triggering this—and then get to the bottom of it!

Chapters 2 and 3 on emotional intelligence will help greatly here, and more clues to the cause of their behaviour can be found by applying the Learned Confidence model discussed here (see figure 9.1). This model depicts a pathway for building a competent and confident team and shows the stages people typically go through on their path to *confident competence*.

Figure 9.1: the Learned Confidence model

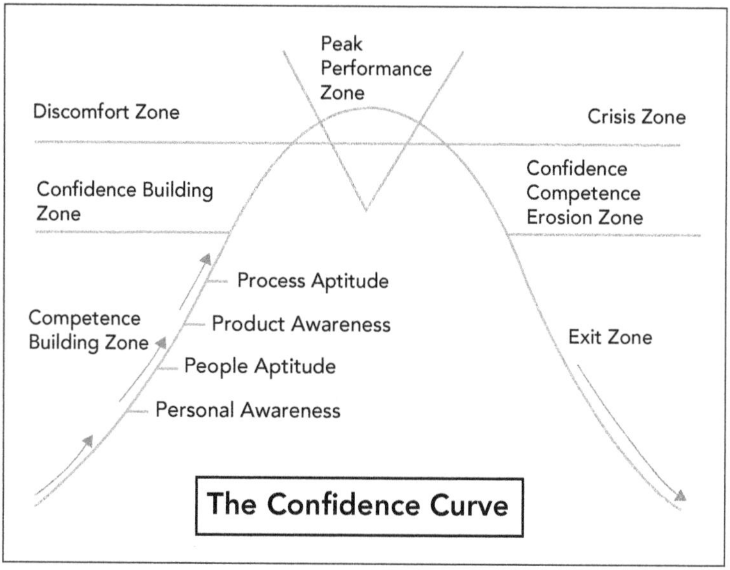

The Confidence Curve depicted in figure 9.1 identifies four areas of knowledge that people need to address on their journey towards confidence. We call this the confidence-building zone, and the activities that a manager must concentrate on with their team members are the '4 PA's':

- personal awareness
- people aptitude
- product awareness
- process aptitude.

Personal awareness

Personal awareness must always be the starting point to any work on building confidence. As we have discussed, to grow in confidence people must understand *themselves* and what makes them tick, as well as how others perceive them, in order to pinpoint the specific behaviours they need to work on.

As a manager, you must use clever, thought-provoking questioning to help your people uncover exactly what is blocking their growth in confidence. Your questions should aim to uncover any personal skills or behaviours that are lacking, any personal beliefs that may be blocking or eroding their confidence, or any negative impressions they may have of how others see them.

You should be aware there is a strong correlation between self-awareness and confidence. People who are self-aware typically know what they are and are not good at and what their triggers are.

This exercise in itself will serve to increase confidence levels immediately. Now add a plan to bridge the identified gaps and you will launch your team member successfully on their journey.

People aptitude

The second PA stems from the ability of your people to demonstrate and build their understanding of others (empathy) and to interact appropriately with them to achieve the desired results.

They need to be finely attuned to what makes others tick. As this aptitude increases, the likelihood of your people misunderstanding or upsetting others or not meeting client needs will diminish—and with this will come an increase in confidence.

Share your learnings on empathy and what makes people tick from chapter 5 to help your people build their skills around understanding others. This is a vital step in building confidence in your team. As they deal with people every day and as their personal interaction and communication improves, so will their confidence.

As you can see, these first two elements are closely aligned to the learnings in this book around understanding the self and others. The next two elements are organisation specific and also relate to learnings earlier in the book. They bear on a knowledge of the products or services that employees work with *and* the application of processes and procedures.

Product awareness

As discussed at length in Part II, your people must be well versed in the organisation's products whether or not their job technically requires it. You must train your people to understand every aspect of your products, including what features they offer and what needs they meet.

This product engagement is vital in any organisation. Where there is high product engagement there is confidence, and where there is confidence there is increased influence and sales, better decision making, more creativity and higher levels of innovation.

Process aptitude

The final piece of the puzzle for building confidence is helping your people to achieve confidence in applying the organisational processes and procedures. You must continually coach, train and assess your people in their process and procedure application. The more time you spend on this, the more confident your people will become and the better they will perform.

Most organisations set aside time in the induction phase to do this fairly well. Where it falls down is during the post-induction period, when reinforcement is often lacking and people are left to 'find their own way'. During this phase organisations typically rely on other team members to help out in conveying information. This can be damaging as messages are diluted or distorted when necessary steps are left out during the transfer of information, either being forgotten, taken for granted or rushed through—all of which can result in a 'Chinese whispers' effect.

Effective plans must be in place to ensure your processes and procedure are being reinforced correctly. Think about who you can use as champions in your team to maintain consistency in communication. This will take time in the beginning, but it will save you a huge amount in the end—and you will have built a confident, productive team.

Once you have trained your people in these elements, the competence they achieve will guarantee that their confidence will grow too.

From here your people can follow either one of two pathways. Which path they take will wholly depend on the mindsets of your people—and in most cases on *your* level of support. There are those who will be happy to plateau and coast along at the competent level, and then there are those who will want to progress to the zone of high performance.

For most, this will require that they again move out of their competence zone and into a zone of discomfort.

As they move through this zone they will need to be guided as there will be risk involved—and with risk, we know, comes fear. Your job is to influence the mindset of your high performer by understanding exactly what they need from you—and delivering it!

Once your high performer reaches the zone of peak performance, you both start to reap the rewards. The zone of peak performance is where creativity, innovation and profits lie. This is the key to progress and *sustained* organisation and team performance.

It is not realistic to expect all of your people to reach this stage. In fact, such an outcome is not recommended, as within every team you need A players and B players. Your job is to guide your high-performing team member when they need it, and to offer encouragement and feedback and enough of a push to keep them there.

Remember, this is an intricate process in which everyone is progressing at a different rate. If you push people too hard, they may become daunted, lose confidence and slip backwards—or even go over the edge. If you don't push hard enough then complacency can set in and they can lose interest. The right level of tension or pressure is required, and only you will know what level that should be, based on your empathy skills.

What is really exciting about this zone is that it is also the zone of hidden potential. It is where competent and confident people realise new or hidden skills, and it should be every manager's dream to help uncover such potential. It is where the intricate balance of tension, support, challenge and individual desire facilitates the unlocking of potential, and when all these forces converge or align, startling results can be achieved.

Finally, the confidence erosion zone, the zone where no one wants to find themselves, is where the intricate balance is lost. This typically starts in the crisis zone when an individual is pushed too fast or too hard. Quite often it is related to burnout.

More often than not, however, it has its source in external problems related to some kind of change affecting the organisation itself or the individual's direct manager. Examples include a change in CEO, a change in company direction or products, or a manager losing interest in communicating, coaching, guiding and mentoring their teams effectively.

To create a team of confident mindsets a manager must always be thinking along the following lines:

- My first job is to build a competent team.

- With competence comes confidence.

- Confidence comes from knowledge and awareness of self, people, products and process.

- Confidence unlocks the potential in people.

- It is my job to unlock potential in others.

- Confidence breeds innovation and creativity.

- Confidence is critical to performance sustainability.

- Influence increases as confidence increases.

- People 'buy' ideas and products from confident people.

- Assets of a confident and competent team are pride, satisfaction, engagement and connection.

A manager also needs to be aware of the common barriers to confidence. Existing mindsets will need to be overcome, influenced or managed. These usually become evident when people:

- say they are not 'naturally confident' or 'it's something you're born with and I wasn't'

- need things spelt out and are not comfortable with any type of ambiguity

- don't speak up in meetings as they are afraid they may be shown up

- continually say they need more training

- constantly check in to see if they are on the right track

- appear to be naturally confident and able to wing their way through most things

- boast/overcompensate/take over in front of others.

The information in this chapter should assist you in overcoming these barriers to identify exactly where confidence is lacking in your team, why it is absent and how to fill the gap.

Chapter summary

■ Confidence is an essential element in the make-up of the high performer. It allows them to grow and pursue new skills.

■ A lack of confidence in a team member usually derives from a lack of aptitude or awareness of some sort.

■ Use the Learned Confidence model to pinpoint the cause of any negative or unusual behaviour in a team member.

■ There are four areas of knowledge or awareness in the confidence-building zone. They are:

➤ personal awareness

➤ people aptitude

➤ product awareness

➤ process aptitude.

■ Letting people 'find their own way' will be costly in the long run, as any information passed informally among team members can rapidly become diluted or distorted.

■ Once your team has acquired competence there will be those who are happy to coast at this level and those who want to progress to the zone of high performance. Which path they take depends wholly on the mindsets of your people and your willingness to help them get there.

■ When developing a high performer, your job is to guide them when they need it, offering encouragement, feedback and enough of a push to get them to the next level and keep them there.

■ Be alert for confidence erosion, which can occur when an individual is pushed too fast or too hard.

- High performers will eventually disengage if their manager leaves them too long without attention.

- A by-product of a confident and competent team is pride, which is one of the best employee engagement drivers.

Reflective questions

1. Evaluate where you currently personally sit on the performance curve and suggest reasons why.

2. Which of the 4 PA's are you weakest in?

3. How does this impact your team?

4. Out of 10, how would your team rate you in terms of confidence?

5. Why would this be the case?

6. Identify why you are or are not in the zone of high performance.

7. What could cause your confidence to erode?

8. How well do you actively support your high achievers?

9. Out of 10, how proud would you say your team is?

Where to start

1. Guide your people onto the confidence curve and identify what development they need to become truly competent. Then work this into their performance planning process.

2. Identify people on your team who have competence in key areas and train them to coach the other team members. This task should be delegated but you still need to drive it. Hand over responsibility but retain accountability.

3. Identify promptly who in your team are in the crisis zone and plan an approach perhaps involving your HR department. These are the people you could be about to lose and who can negatively influence others in your team.

4. Identify those of your people who are in the high-performance zone and devise a plan to ensure you give them what they need in terms of recognition, support and resources. *Do not forget* these people. They too are at a critical point at which they could decide to go elsewhere where they feel more appreciated!

chapter 10

The manager as trainer—how to share knowledge and train your team quickly

Now we understand how people build competence and confidence, we need to focus on the mindset and skills required to develop the capabilities of our people in the context of their ongoing growth.

For ongoing growth to happen, there *must* be learning. Even if your organisation is not committed to learning, as a manager you must find ways to help your team grow in knowledge, competence and performance.

There are numerous ways to do this. Many of them are very straightforward to implement and do not require you to spend years qualifying as a trainer.

As a specialist in management and adult education with many years' experience, I now know there are shortcuts, and this chapter is dedicated to sharing these with you. I have chosen the best eight tips and techniques to enable you to up-skill quickly to facilitate learning in your team. From here all you need is a bit of imagination and, above all, the mindset to *want* your people to learn.

Before we begin, though, let's look at some of the ways learning occurs within an organisation or team.

Typically, learning will occur when an organisation or manager:

- sets stretch goals and assignments
- coaches and mentors their team formally or informally
- communicates and shares messages
- ensures people collaborate on a project or task
- encourages people to share ideas and knowledge
- continuously assesses what is going on and makes appropriate changes
- creates a supportive learning environment where people feel comfortable to learn
- establishes concrete learning processes and practices
- provides leadership that reinforces learning
- creates learning opportunities to suit all styles of learners
- facilitates self-driven learning
- rewards self-driven learning
- ensures both formal and informal learning is offered.

The bottom line is that everyone needs to be learning and sharing knowledge, and it is your job to facilitate this. As a manager, you are also a trainer, coach and mentor for your team, which can be no mean feat, especially when most team leaders and managers are not taught how. To do it competently requires an understanding of what adults must have in order to be able to learn, what the different styles of adult learners are, how to build a training session and how to deliver a training session.

So how do you achieve this? How can you build and deliver a training session? How can you create a learning culture within your team? The following eight tips should help you.

Tips on adult learning

Tip 1: Understand adult learners

The first thing you must understand is that the adult learning mindset operates completely differently from the learning mindset of a child. Children are typically open-minded towards new learning. An adult's ability and inclination to learn will depend very much on how they *feel*.

You should also understand that adult learners are problem or performance centred, which means they must see how learning will either solve a problem for them or help them perform. In other words, there must be a reward for them.

Another vital clue to understanding the mindset of the adult learner is that they fear failure or looking stupid. If they do not feel comfortable, not only will they not learn but they can also feel threatened and potentially become disruptive.

So to be able to learn, an adult needs:

• to feel safe with you and the environment

• to understand the 'why' of the learning

• to be involved in the process

• to be offered different ways to learn

• to be able to use their own experience as a foundation for new information

• to be convinced, as their point of view will often be set

• to be ready to learn.

Now we understand a bit about adult learners, let's look at how they tend to learn.

Tip 2: Understand how adults learn

When thinking about how adults learn it is important to know that there are *visual learners, auditory learners* and *kinaesthetic learners*. These three predominant learning styles are commonly referred to as VAK Learning Styles. Adults learn by using all three styles, but you will find that one style will usually be dominant in most people.

Understanding and accommodating the different learning styles will help you prepare to coach, mentor and train your team. As George Evans once said, 'Every student has the ability to learn—just not on the same day, or in the same way'. So let's examine these learning styles in more detail.

Visual learners

The visual learning style involves observation—of people and things, including pictures, diagrams, demonstrations, displays, handouts, films and flipcharts.

How to spot a person with a preference for visual learning

- They tend to be neat and orderly at home and at work.

- They tend to speak quickly.

- They are very observant and tend to notice small details.

- They are appearance oriented in both dress and presentation.

- They are good spellers and can see the words in their minds.

- They memorise by visual association.

- They tend to have good handwriting.

- They may forget verbal instructions such as directions unless they're written down.

- They are usually fast, strong readers.

Auditory learners

The auditory learning style involves the transfer of information through listening, speech, sounds and noises.

How to spot a person with a preference for auditory learning

- They learn by listening and remember what was said rather than what they have seen.

- They can be easily distracted by noise.

- They like to hear someone explain something.

- They are frequently eloquent speakers.

- They are talkative, love discussion and will go into lengthy descriptions.

- They like music more than art and tend to be great at remembering lyrics.

Kinaesthetic learners

The kinaesthetic learning style involves the transfer of information through physical experience. This includes touching, feeling, holding, doing and hands-on experiences.

How to spot a person with a preference for kinaesthetic learning

- They like to learn by doing and being 'hands on'.

- They use action words in their speech.

- They tend to be quite tactile with people.

- They tend to be physically oriented, move a lot and can't sit still for long periods of time.

- They like to make things.

- They tend not to enjoy reading.

- They wave their hands or gesture when talking.

Now you understand how adults learn, you will need to keep in mind how to ensure you engage all types of learners in your training sessions.

So let's take a look at how you will do this.

You must understand there are two parts to this—first, actually building a presentation and second, turning your presentation into a training session. This is the easiest way for managers to prepare for training.

Tip 3: The easiest way to build a presentation (part 1)

How to build a presentation in six easy steps.

Step 1: Identify aims and objectives (the most important part of the design process)	• What is the goal of the presentation? • What must my team learn? • How much time do I have to cover the information?
Step 2: Research information to share	• What do I already know about this topic? • What do I need to learn about this topic? • Where can I access the knowledge I need?
Step 3: Brainstorm what I will need to include (use a mind map to get information out of your head and onto paper!)	• What do I need to include and how much detail is required? • How will I achieve my aims?
Step 4: Structure and build framework	• Now I have all my ideas on paper, how will I organise and prioritise the content using PowerPoint? • Make a slide for each section heading and arrange the headings in logical order.
Step 5: Add content	• Now add the content. Don't check it as you go—just get the information on your slides and in the right sections.
Step 6: Review logic and flow	• Now review the content. Are the sections logical in approach and order? • Is the flow of information easy to follow and sequential? • Does the organisation make sense?

Tip 4: How to turn a presentation into a basic training session (part 2)

Turn your presentation into a training session and create an adult learning experience.

Two-part focus	In tip 3 we concentrated on how to put a presentation together based on CONTENT, FACT and THEORY. To turn the presentation into a training session, you now need to focus on LEARNING, APPEAL and INTEREST.
Ensure knowledge retention	During the session: • Your ultimate goal is to ensure knowledge retention and application. • To achieve this, ensure your adult learners are actively involved in the learning. • Do mini exercises to test learning application. • Ensure your adult learners feel comfortable with you.
Training techniques	Use a variety of training techniques to accommodate visual, auditory and kinaesthetic styles of adult learners such as: • brainstorming ideas on a whiteboard • demonstrating how to do things • roleplaying • discussion and debate • games.
Training tools and methods	Use a variety of training tools to keep learners engaged and interested, such as: • computers • handouts • cards • posters • books • whiteboard • games • software.

Now you have a sense of how you will run your session you need to create a lesson plan to ensure you achieve your aims and objectives, use lots of variety in the delivery of your session—and do all of this in the time allotted.

Tip 5: How to create a learning plan

A learning plan helps you plan how you will deliver the information, how long you will spend on each section and what variety of tools you will use to ensure learning is achieved—and your session is kept on track.

Use the template below.

Summary	Time	Tool	Outline and technique

Tip 6: Personal preparation

Preparation and practice are everything. You cannot 'wing it' with training. It needs thorough preparation on many levels because your credibility will hinge on this.

So you need to make sure you know your material thoroughly before you deliver your session. Practise in front of a mirror or record yourself on your phone or tablet and play it back to see how you come across. This will help you build confidence.

Always make sure your opening is strong and will hook in your team. Remember, adult learners need to know what's in it for them, and a good hook will help you identify this.

Anticipate the likely questions your team will ask and prepare some possible answers ahead of time.

Always make sure you keep eye contact with your people and engage them in the learning as much as possible.

Finally, ensure ahead of time that the technology you are using works and is ready to go, so your confidence is not undermined just as you are about to start!

Tip 7: Informal learning — it doesn't always need to be so formal!

As a starting point, make reading non-negotiable! The fact is most people love to learn. The truth, however, is that often what gets dropped first in our fast-paced world is business- or work-related reading.

If your people are not studying, then they should be reading. They need to know what is going in their field, who is who, who is doing what, and the latest knowledge and trends. If this is not happening, then naturally you must be the catalyst to spark their interest and drive the uptake of this essential knowledge.

Knowledge powers inspiration, ideas and creativity — the essential ingredients so often missing in teams today. You must facilitate an environment in which minds are kept open and existing mindsets are challenged. If you want to drive a high-performance culture your business must be rooted in learning. Encourage it and do it yourself. Set a trend and be a role model — it always starts with you!

Tip 8: Fun learning ideas and social media

If your meetings are boring (as most are), incorporate an element of knowledge sharing. Allocate a week to each team member to talk about what they have learned recently that they can share with their team mates.

Start a team book club! Choose one book per quarter, then work out a time frame and structure for your team to read individual chapters and report back. Think creatively about how you can visually share learnings, quotes and ideas from the book in your office. Use a whiteboard or flipchart paper bluetacked to the wall (if you don't have a whiteboard, flipchart or stand).

Encourage people to bring in articles they have read and post them online or on a pinboard in your office. Get people to add thoughts and ideas on Post-it notes on the printed article or virtually online.

Who's who? Get your people interested in who are the movers and shakers in your industry or profession. Acknowledge them in the office and learn about them; again get your people to do the research and then share their findings in team meetings. They could use Pinterest or Tumblr to post their faces along with a short blurb on who they are and what they have achieved.

These ideas will drive individual inspiration, motivation, collaboration and pride within your team. Watch as those who were less interested in the beginning soon get involved for fear of being left out or left behind!

Chapter summary

- The adult learning mindset operates completely differently from the learning mindset of a child. Children are typically open-minded towards new learning. An adult's ability and inclination to learn will depend very much on how they *feel*.

- An adult needs to feel safe with you and the environment, to understand the 'why' of the learning, to be involved in the process, to be offered different ways to learn, to be able to use their own experience as a foundation for new information and to be convinced, as their point of view will often be set.

- Identifying the aims and objectives of your training session will determine its quality and the time you will spend putting it together.

- Before you start, ask yourself: How much do they already know? What do they need to learn? How much time do I have?

- To generate content for your training session, brainstorm ideas, ask yourself key questions and use a mind map.

- When using PowerPoint, don't labour the different points of your session too much initially as you generate content. You may change your mind down the track. The process should be fluid as priorities may change.

- Remember, adult learners need to get involved in the training session to retain the knowledge. Variety is key!

- Training tools and techniques are essential to turn your presentation into a learning experience.

- Don't forget to have fun with social media to encourage learning in your team!

Reflective questions

1. Think about your last training session—what went well?

2. What didn't go well and why?

3. How do you know that your team actually learned what you set out to teach them?

4. Provide examples to prove that your session was a training session, not merely a presentation.

5. Review what you could have done to ensure your team learned more effectively.

6. Reflect on the structure and logic of the session—did it flow seamlessly?

7. Write down the steps you went through in putting the session together.

8. Compare these steps with the steps outlined in this chapter.

9. How engaged was your team? How do you know?

10. What would you do differently next time?

Where to start

1. Make a plan to help your team learn and grow in knowledge, competence and performance. Be creative in your ideas and have fun with it.

2. Encourage individuals and the team as a whole to reflect on and analyse the way they behave and do things.

3. Create learning opportunities to suit all styles of learners, including visual, auditory and kinaesthetic.

4. Remember, when developing a training session preparation and practice are key. Ask yourself: How much do they already know? What do they need to learn? How much time do I have? How can I ensure they will understand, learn and retain what I teach them?

chapter 11

How learners think and how to adapt your style

Many years ago I came across a wonderful tool for understanding what makes people tick and how they think—and therefore learn. Based on the work of Ned Herrmann, the Herrmann Brain Thinking Styles Profile tool provides us with an illuminating model and metaphor for how people think, connect and learn.

The *whole brain thinking* concept evolved from the early research of scientists Roger Sperry and Paul McLean, who made startling discoveries relating to the evolution and functionality of the brain. In particular, Sperry popularised the notion of the 'left brain' and 'right brain' and went on to describe how people have natural tendencies and preferences relating to one side or the other (see figure 11.1, overleaf).

Figure 11.1: Sperry's left-brain/right-brain theory

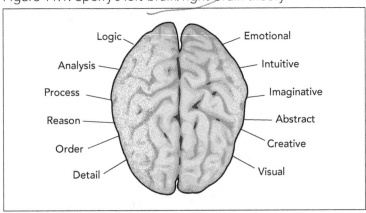

Those who are 'left brained', he found, draw on natural tendencies relating to logic, analysis and process. Left-brain thinkers collect information using logic and reason. Their brain processes are deductive, rational, concrete and analytically based. Information is retained using words, numbers and symbols.

Left-brain thinkers and learners express themselves concisely though words, numerical and written formulas, and technological systems. Processing each element of an idea guides them in their logical, step-by-step gathering of information.

Left-brain thinkers see only parts of an idea. Right-brain thinkers, conversely, see the whole concept.

People use functions from both sides of their brain to accomplish most tasks in their daily lives. There are some nonverbal tasks, such as drawing, painting, dancing and music, in which our right brain excels. Right-brained people gather information through feelings and intuition, drawing on their emotions, relationships and creativity.

Right-brain thinkers and learners are able to visualise the whole idea as they compile their research. Their thought processes may sometimes appear illogical and disjointed because they are emotional, intuitive, abstract and laterally connected. Analysis of this information or problem solving often involves free association, and while the solution may be innovative, the route travelled to reach this conclusion might be impossible for a more logical, left-brain thinker to follow.

Visual thinkers do not use a step-by-step process to accumulate information; rather, it is visually grasped all at once, which makes organisation of this information and conveying the data, either in written or verbal form, difficult. Right-brain thinkers are best able to express themselves using images and patterns, music or dance.

To connect, teach, train, coach or mentor people successfully, you need to deliver information to them in ways that best suit their thinking processes. I use this idea in everything I do, from selling and customer service to leading, managing and teaching. However, there is more to it than just two styles of thinkers and learners.

In fact, Ned Herrmann was uncomfortable with this narrow, binary view and his work went on to indicate that there are also two very distinct types of people who are 'left brained' and two very distinct types who are 'right brained', producing a simple four-component model (see figure 11.2, overleaf).

Figure 11.2: the Whole Brain® model

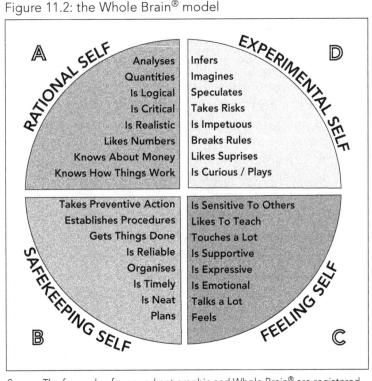

Source: The four-color, four-quadrant graphic and Whole Brain® are registered trademarks of Herrmann Global LLC. The Whole Brain® Model is © 2014 Herrmann Global LLC. Used with permission. For more information regarding the Whole Brain® Model and the Herrmann Brain Dominance Instrument® used to assess thinking style preferences, please visit www.herrmannsolutions.com.

What this model shows is that there are four types of people who think in a certain way and therefore communicate and process information in a certain way—which is vital for learning and growth. Let's have a look at each and see how they apply to how you will communicate, train, coach and mentor.

The A quadrant — known as the blue thinking preference

The first thing to remember as you read through the descriptions and implications of these styles is that each of your team members is capable of accessing all four thinking styles. We are talking here about preference or inclination, *not* competence. What this means is that we are naturally drawn to certain styles of thinking and learning over others, but we are capable of all of them.

People who incline to the blue thinking style tend to prefer to think in terms of facts and numbers. They apply logic to everything they do and take a realistic approach to their work. When they speak you may hear them say, 'Let's cut to the chase. What's the bottom line?' or 'Just give me the facts'.

These people can be perceived as serious and somewhat critical and blunt in their delivery. They are often intimidating, level-headed under pressure and, at times, cold.

Blue thinkers become frustrated with people who they think are overly emotional, who are unable to articulate their ideas clearly or who don't provide figures to validate an idea.

So what does this mean?

- The number one rule for communicating successfully with your blue thinkers is to deliver information to them in a clear, concise way and to back it up with proof. Technical accuracy is essential to your blue people.

- Take time to think about how you will explain and articulate complex situations, as they will likely get frustrated if you don't make sense. Avoid any emotional language or chitchat.

- Set clear goals and objectives and show how everything fits together to help your blue thinker perform to their highest level.

The B quadrant — known as the green thinking preference

The green thinking preference represents those who are driven by safety, process and procedure. These people tend to be comfortable with high levels of detail, are usually neat in the way they work and can be relied on to get things done. They are also great goal setters, action planners and colour coders. They like to work in a methodical, step-by-step way, with contingency plans usually close to hand.

They prefer clear, black-and-white instructions. They are not comfortable with a high degree of ambiguity, prefer to be given exact instructions on how to do something, and need a thorough and complete understanding of what is expected of them.

You will usually hear them request an agenda, argue for keeping meetings on track with minimal digression, and ask for full explanations on how something will work and whether it will follow procedures and protocols.

So what does this mean?

- The number one rule for communicating successfully with your green thinkers is to be precise, timely, organised and prepared.

- Take time to think about how you will explain process and procedure step by step, and always apply logic.

- Ensure you have contingency plans in place, as your green thinkers will be concerned about what could happen if things go awry.

- As far as possible talk with your green thinker in black-and-white terms; loose instructions and ambiguity frustrates them and leads to a lack in confidence.

- Communication and connection differences between green thinkers (the B quadrant) and yellow thinkers (the D quadrant) have proven it to be the second most challenging pairing. There will be tension between great ideas and the practicalities of their implementation.

The C quadrant — known as the red thinking preference

Your red thinkers may stand out as a social breed, very much in touch with other people's feelings and highly intuitive. Red thinkers care about the impact that systems, issues and situations have on people and their feelings.

Natural teachers, these people will be very supportive within the team and possibly the 'go to' people for information. Others will be drawn to the red thinkers, as they tend to make people comfortable and relaxed. They are great at building rapport and are highly empathic in most situations.

Your red thinkers will probably also be quite expressive in their formal and informal communication. They usually prefer a relaxed and friendly environment, as anything too sterile or formal can be perceived as threatening.

You will hear red thinkers ask others how they are feeling. They are affected by things going on around them and can also be quite tactile.

So what does this mean?

- The number one rule for communicating with your red thinkers is to be relaxed and personable in your approach.

- Allow time for discussion and debate to help mutual understanding.

- Don't overuse data or be too critical.

- Build comfort and safety.

- Demonstrate respect and empathy in your communication.

The D quadrant — known as the yellow thinking preference

Finally, your yellow thinkers are those who always seem to come up with the ideas. Playful and often risk takers, these team members love the freedom to explore new concepts and ideas and will want to know how things work, are integrated and come together.

Highly intuitive, these people tend to be very much in touch and up to date with what is newly available. They are early adopters, as new things excite them.

Yellow thinkers tend to be fast thinkers and are sometimes perceived as 'a little out there' by others, as their thinking can be difficult to follow. In turn, they will often challenge the status quo, can quickly be bored by detail, and may not care for too much in the way of rigid processes or timelines.

They typically are interested in 'the big picture' and are likely to incorporate many such metaphors in their speech. Yellow thinkers have a distaste for being categorised or 'put in a box' by models such as this!

So what does this mean?

- The number one rule for communicating successfully with your yellow thinkers is to talk about the future and ideas wherever possible.

- Be fast in your delivery because they can lose interest and get bored very quickly!

- Always talk about the big picture and how everything fits into the long-term strategy.

- Wherever possible use visual imagery and metaphors in your speech.

- Remember, communication and connection differences between green thinkers and yellow thinkers make it the second hardest pairing of all. Pull back on any tendencies to overload the yellow thinker with detail and be prepared to step out of your comfort zone to deliver information in a more creative way.

Now that we understand how people think and process information, this new insight, together with your understanding of how adults learn (see chapter 10), positions you extremely well to facilitate effective learning and growth within your team.

Chapter summary

- The construct of 'left-brain' and 'right-brain' thinking is used to explain how people have natural tendencies and preferences in the way they take in information and devise solutions.

- People are capable of accessing all four thinking styles but everyone inclines towards one style they typically use.

- People who incline to the blue thinking style tend to prefer to think in terms of facts and numbers.

- A blue thinker appreciates being given clear goals and shown how everything fits together.

- Green-thinking people get things done and are great goal setters. They like to complete work in a methodical way, step by step.

- Ensure you have contingency plans in place as a green thinker will be concerned about what could happen if things do not go to plan.

- Red thinkers care about the impact that systems, issues and situations have on people. They are supportive of others and usually the 'go to' people for information.

- When communicating with a red thinker allow time for discussion and debate to help their understanding.

- Yellow thinkers are ideas people. They love having the freedom to explore new concepts and how things work.

- When communicating with a yellow thinker, talk about the future and 'big picture' ideas.

Reflective questions

1. Which thinking style sounds most like you?

2. What clues back this up?

3. What could your second preferred thinking style be?

4. What is the evidence?

5. How do you think your thinking styles impact how you like to process information and therefore how you like to learn?

6. What do you think is your least preferred thinking style and why?

7. How does this thinking style impact your ability to process new information or learn new concepts?

8. Think about a person in your team who has a very different thinking style to yours. Why is it different?

9. How effective do you think you are at communicating, training, coaching and mentoring your team? How do you know?

10. How do you think you could perhaps adapt your coaching or training style to help them learn and pick things up more easily?

Where to start

1. As always look within first. Figure out what your preferred thinking style is before you try to work out others. (The reflective questions will help you here.)

2. Second as always keep your antennae up. Look for all the clues and signals in others that help you understand how they think.

3. In particular look out for clues in how they speak and what questions they ask. This gives you a great insight into what they are thinking and how they absorb information, which you can then use to help them learn and grow.

4. Finally, when your team members seem to lack understanding in something and get frustrated — or have difficulty in retaining information — ask yourself, did you present the information in a way they would understand or in the way you preferred to deliver it?

5. For more information visit www.herrmannsolutions.com or contact us at www.fourmindsets.com.

chapter 12

The manager as coach and mentor — 10 essential tips

A core competency of any manager or team leader today is the ability to coach and mentor their people through a variety of situations. In fact, within most high-performing organisations you simply will not be made a manager unless you have demonstrated an aptitude and desire to coach and mentor others.

Becoming a competent coach and mentor takes time, but you already have many insights into what makes adult learners tick and how to run a basic training session, so now it's about customising your approach further in a one-on-one setting.

To get you up and running, in this chapter we share our 10 best tips to launch you quickly on your journey to becoming an effective coach and mentor.

Tips for coaching and mentoring

Tip 1: Understand what coaching is and isn't!

Coaching is about a relationship in which knowledge and experience are shared between two people in order to develop the learner's skills and to help them carry out their tasks. It is *not* about 'issuing a set of instructions to your people'. Typically, when managers think they are coaching an employee in a task, they are really just downloading information.

Coaching is a structured process that requires preparation similar to that for a basic training session as outlined in the previous chapter. You need to clearly identify your aims and objectives, prepare appropriate resources and, as always, ensure that the learner can see the relevance of what they are learning.

The coaching process can be quite intimidating, as there are usually just the two of you. Your learner or coachee is very much on the spot and can feel very exposed, and this will cause anxiety in an adult learner. So in your preparation think about how you might overcome this potential for fear in your coachee.

Tip 2: Be clear on what coaching brings to a team or organisation — what's in it for you!

Because the coaching process is time consuming, it is typically overlooked and other tasks take priority. It is important for a manager to understand that coaching delivers results on many levels so it is well worth putting time into it and actually scheduling sessions with your team.

Figure 12.1 illustrates the main returns and benefits you can expect from coaching.

Figure 12.1: the benefits of coaching your team

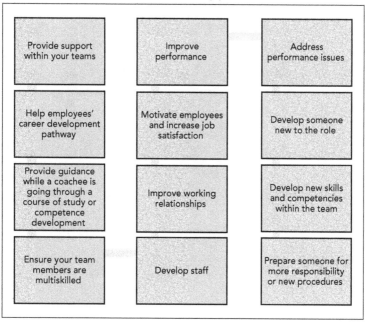

Provide support within your teams	Improve performance	Address performance issues
Help employees' career development pathway	Motivate employees and increase job satisfaction	Develop someone new to the role
Provide guidance while a coachee is going through a course of study or competence development	Improve working relationships	Develop new skills and competencies within the team
Ensure your team members are multiskilled	Develop staff	Prepare someone for more responsibility or new procedures

Tip 3: Be clear on what the mindset of a coach entails

We have talked at length throughout this book about the mindsets and skills required to manage a team. The same mindsets apply to coaching. Figure 12.2 (overleaf) identifies the most commonly cited skills, behaviours and mindsets required to become a competent coach.

Figure 12.2: top 10 core coaching skills and behaviours

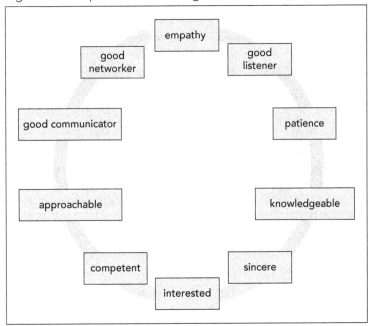

As an effective coach you must be mindful of what each of these elements means from a coaching perspective:

1. *empathy*—the key ability for understanding and anticipating how your coachee sees things

2. *good listener*—the number one asset for every coach, who should say little and ask questions

3. *patience*—to let the coachee offer solutions to issues without you jumping in first to solve the problem for them

4. *knowledgeable*—ensuring you are up to date in your knowledge so you are able to share relevant points of view

5. *sincere*—with a genuine desire to help your people

6. *interested*—being 100 per cent in the moment when coaching, not disrupted by emails, phone calls or other interruptions

7. *competent*—speaks for itself!

8. *approachable*—making sure your coachee feels safe and comfortable to approach you and ask you questions

9. *good communicator*—ensuring you can articulate well and not interrupting or speaking over your coachee or making them feel uncomfortable

10. *good networker*—like all the best coaches, knowing to whom to refer your people for further help in their learning.

Tip 4: Use the 6-Step Coaching model when coaching someone on how to perform a task

This model offers a useful template to apply when coaching someone on how to perform a wide variety of simple process tasks, such as raising an invoice or entering information on a system.

The first step is to explain why the task is important. Why are you having this session? Describe how the task fits into the big picture. Where appropriate, bring a sample of the finished product or process to show the learner.

Step 2 is to demonstrate the task at normal speed. Ask the learner not to ask any questions at this stage so the task can be shown uninterrupted.

Step 3 is to demonstrate the task again, this time slowly, explaining each stage. Ask the learner to watch carefully and write down any questions they might have, but not to ask them until you have finished your demonstration.

In step 4 reverse roles, letting the learner walk you through the process slowly, asking for help when needed. Encourage them as they move through the task. Stop them when they do something incorrectly and explain how to do it properly. Ask them to explain the tasks they are carrying out so you can assess their understanding and whether there are any gaps in their knowledge.

In step 5, allow the learner time to practise. Repetition and practice are vital to their learning.

Finally, in step 6, assess their performance of the task and give feedback and offer praise and recognition where due.

Tip 5: Use the GROW model for coaching people who want to change a behaviour or develop in some way

The GROW model is one of the most popular coaching models used globally and can also be used very effectively as a questioning model in problem solving processes.

A CEO once told me that of all the things he had learned over the years, this was the one model he had never forgotten. He actually still uses it every day when dealing with his managers and senior leadership team.

The model serves well as a discussion framework to identify what a person needs to *grow* and develop, but it can also be used very successfully in decision making.

The four steps are:

Goals—What are your goals? What do you want to achieve?

Reality—What is the current reality? What is happening right now?

Options—What are your options? What could you do?

Will—What will you do? What have you decided to do?

Tip 6: Be AWESOME at asking questions

We have noted throughout the book that as a manager you must be *great* at asking questions—it is a key management skill. Being able to dig for information and to keep an open mind before making decisions will serve you well.

To hone your skills with the GROW model and help you develop your questioning skills in general, go to www.fourmindsets.com for supplementary lists of questions you should consider asking.

Tip 7: Understand the difference between coaching and mentoring

Many people do not understand the difference between mentoring and coaching, as the roles can overlap. Most managers today are expected to carry out both roles. The common differences between the two can be summarised as follows.

Managers coach staff as a required part of their job, the coaching taking place within a formal employment relationship. Mentoring occurs, by mutual consent, often outside the line manager/ employee relationship. Its focus is outside the mentee's immediate area of work on their broader career.

Managers focus on developing individuals within their current roles; the interest of the relationship is functional. Mentoring relationships cross job boundaries. A mentor provides both professional and personal support; the relationship is more personal.

Managers tend to initiate and drive the coaching relationship. Mentoring relationships may be initiated by mentors or created by an organisation matching process.

The coaching relationship ends when the coachee has learned what the coach is teaching. Mentoring relationships typically last for a specific time period.

Tip 8: Understand what it means to be a mentor

The Oxford School of Coaching and Mentoring's Eric Pasloe defines mentoring as:

> to support and encourage people to manage their own learning in order that they may maximise their potential,

develop their skills, improve their performance and become the person they want to be.

As you develop your management skills there will come a time when you will be required to mentor other people. When this happens the following definitions will serve you well to keep you on track with your objectives as a mentor.

Mentoring can be used to:

- solve a people-related issue

- provide career advice, such as helping a team member to determine their next step and what training they may need to reach their goal

- help a team member achieve and maintain a satisfactory work–life balance

- help resolve a conflict or potential conflict within the team.

Mentoring benefits include:

- improved decision-making capability

- development of talent pool or succession plan

- demonstration of personal and professional standards

- establishing a learning pathway

- fostering a learning organisation

- developing cross-organisational networks.

Tip 9: How to be a good storyteller

As a mentor, it will help you to use a story in different situations to convey information or illustrate a point. There are five main types of stories that you can use in the workplace.

'Who am I' stories

Use this type of story when you have a new team member, or if you have taken on a new team. Your team will be keen to understand what you will be like to work with, so tell them about yourself! This approach helps to break down walls and gives your team the chance to understand who you are as a person and manager. Use this story to show you are human and approachable.

'Why I'm here' stories

The reason for telling this story is to help your team to understand what your goals are and what you hope to achieve. This will help build trust by showing transparency.

Teaching stories

A teaching story is a story of how you learned a valuable lesson at some point in your life or at work. This type of story can be inspirational; it may also serve to help people avoid the same mistake(s) you might have made.

Vision stories

These stories remind everyone of what the ultimate goal is, and why it's important that everyone contribute to reaching that goal. This type of story should be compelling and inspirational, told from your heart—and with emotion.

'I know what you're thinking' stories

This is a great story to tell if you are able to predict and anticipate ahead of time that your people may not be happy about a particular situation. If you know how your people are going to think and feel you can tell a story that will help them to overcome these negative thoughts and feelings. Your story must help them to understand why something has to be done in a certain way.

Tip 10: Finally — how people process information

In the previous chapter we looked at what makes adult learners tick. Before you start coaching and mentoring, you should also take account of how adult learners process information. This should again remind you of the importance of delivering your information in a variety of ways, no matter what the setting.

As a general rule, adult learners remember:

- 10 per cent of what they read
- 20 per cent of what they hear
- 30 per cent of what they see
- 50 per cent of what they see and hear
- 80 per cent of what they say
- 90 per cent of what they say while they are doing the task.

Chapter summary

- Adult learners process information in a variety of ways, so you should have a range of options for how to deliver your coaching session.

- Coaching is a structured process that requires preparation. You need to clearly identify your objectives, prepare appropriate resources and ensure that the person being coached can see the relevance of what they are learning.

- As a manager, you should understand that coaching delivers results on many levels and it is well worth scheduling sessions with your team.

- A good coach demonstrates empathy, is a good listener, has patience and is knowledgeable, sincere, interested, competent, approachable, and a good communicator and networker.

- When coaching someone in how to perform a task, use the 6-Step Coaching model.

- When coaching people who want to change a behaviour or grow in some way, use the GROW model.

- Through asking the right questions, you will be able to isolate an issue and gain agreement and commitment from the person you are coaching to a course of action to resolve it.

- Understand the difference between coaching and mentoring, and which approach is the most suitable for a given situation.

- When mentoring, use a story to convey information or illustrate a point.

- Adult learners process information in a variety of ways, so you should have a range of options for how to deliver your information.

- Becoming a competent coach and mentor takes time, so always be working on your skills.

Reflective questions

1. When did you last conduct a formal coaching session with a team member?

2. Out of 10, rate how that session went?

3. What was good about the session?

4. What part of the session needed improving?

5. What was the evidence to suggest this was the case?

6. Using the top 10 skills and behaviours for a coach, rank your effectiveness from most effective to least effective.

7. Analyse whether your weaker areas relate to coaching skills or people skills.

8. How will you build capability in your weaker areas?

9. Who else in your team has the potential ability to help you coach?

10. How will you up-skill them to enable them to do this?

Where to start

1. Put a coaching plan in place so that you spend time coaching each of your staff over a given period of time. This will also serve to connect you with your team at a much deeper level.

2. Use the 6-Step Coaching model when coaching someone in how to perform a task.

3. Use the GROW model for coaching people who want to change a behaviour or grow or develop in some way.

4. Use stories to connect with your team and to illustrate a point or convey information in a more compelling way.

Part IV

The Performance Mindset

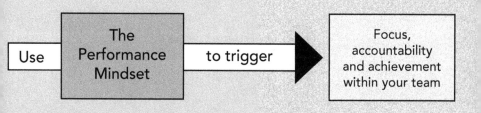

Use	The Performance Mindset	to trigger	Focus, accountability and achievement within your team

In this Part:

➤ How to recruit the right people into your team

➤ The 90-day critical period—how to attach and align your people

➤ How to increase focus and accountability

➤ How to conduct a best practice performance review

chapter 13

How to recruit the right people into your team

The key to managing performance is to make sure you recruit the right people with the right skills and the *right mindset* in the first place, to get 'the right people on the bus' as Jim Collins put it in *Good to Great.*

A study of 5247 hiring managers conducted by Leadership IQ revealed an alarming failure rate among newly hired employees. According to the report, published in the *Harvard Business Review,* respondents collectively hired more than 20 000 employees during the three-year research period. Within 18 months 46 per cent were found to have failed while only 19 per cent achieved success.

The study also found that 26 per cent of new hires fail because they can't accept feedback, 23 per cent cannot understand and manage emotions, 17 per cent lack the drive to succeed, 15 per cent have the wrong temperament and 11 per cent lack the key skills required for the role.

But the primary reason for failure was attributed to 'poor interpersonal skills', which 82 per cent of managers admitted to having *overlooked in the hiring process.*

If people without the required skills are being hired, it is because the interview process is not being conducted effectively. How you interview candidates and their referees is crucial to ensuring you recruit the right people.

Global research continually validates the conclusion that the most effective way of selecting the right candidate is to conduct a behavioural interview. Yet around half of the managers surveyed were not able to describe what a behavioural interview is, let alone how to conduct one.

So what exactly is a behavioural interview?

A behavioural interview focuses on fact rather than hypothesis or 'what if?' situations. It is designed to find out how a future employee actually has behaved in a work-related situation in the past, rather than relying on their own estimation of how they would behave in a future situation.

The behavioural interview does much more than this, however. Its core purpose and objectives can be summarised as to:

- carry out a structured and goal-oriented process

- assist the manager in making a decision not based solely on gut feeling and intuition

- identify past behaviours that will give clues as to what future behaviours can be expected

- gain as much objective data as possible from a subjective assessment method

- carry out a systematic process rather than pose a set of questions

- collect examples of situations that can be further validated during the reference checking phase.

So where should you start?

To carry out a successful behavioural interview, first you must collect all the relevant paperwork. Although this may seem obvious, in our experience elements of this vital step are often skipped, which results in employees who do not match the organisation in terms of either skills, experience, attitude and behaviour.

The paperwork you should collect includes the role advertisement, screening documents, job description, list of behavioural competencies, list of skill-based competencies and key performance indicators required for the job, and the applicant's paperwork. The aim here is to re-examine this paperwork objectively to see if there is something you might hitherto have overlooked and to highlight areas of importance. Remember, the interview is your last chance to address any of these areas.

The next step is to decide if the interview is the only selection method you are going to use or if there are any other evaluation methodologies you could adopt. Typically, the interview contributes about 70 per cent of the information required to make a decision. The other 30 per cent will come from other evaluation methods. These should validate your decision and can serve to challenge your assumptions or perceptions.

The final stage is to decide who will be involved in the interview, and where and when it will be conducted.

Begin by thinking about who will be conducting the interview. Are you handling it alone or will this be a panel interview? If you are doing it alone, who will meet the person at the next stage? If it is being conducted by a panel, who else is going to be involved and why? Do they have all the paperwork required? Are they briefed on what you are looking for? Are they briefed on their role on the panel? Do they understand how to record and evaluate the candidate's responses?

Secondly, where you conduct the interview will send a clear message about your organisation. Choose a quiet, professional, clean and tidy environment where you will not be interrupted. Ensure instructions are clear on where the interview will be held and that the candidate is greeted on arrival. Remember, first impressions are 'moments of truth' and you need to control them. You never know whether the person you are about to meet is going to be your star candidate, so you have to be prepared to ensure they start building the right perceptions about you and the organisation. This is also the first part of the attachment process, which we will cover in the next chapter.

If you are conducting the interview during normal working hours, be conscious of the time constraints on the candidate, especially if it takes place during their lunch break. Ensure the interview does not run over time as this causes stress and anxiety and will affect their performance.

Now you are ready to start the behavioural interview process. It is advisable to go over the process several times to ensure you are familiar with it prior to meeting the candidates. Most people don't do this, instead leaving it to the last minute and then winging it—another reason for many wrong hires.

Let's now look at the what it takes to conduct a best practice behavioural interview. The five steps involved are to analyse the job, develop structured questions, conduct the interview, rank responses and evaluate results.

Step 1: Analyse the job

The goal of this stage is to identify the competencies needed for success in the role. The first set of competencies usually focuses on technical ability; the second set identifies the behaviours required to fulfil the role. These are commonly referred to as *soft skills* or *people skills*. To evaluate these you must think carefully about the differing styles of the people with whom the new recruit will interact.

Another helpful exercise is to analyse a high performer in the role and determine what distinguishes this person from an average performer in terms of skills, behaviours and attitude.

Also, stop and think about any aspect of the role that is unusual.

Step 2: Develop structured questions

The four types of questions are theoretical questions, behavioural questions, leading questions and open questions.

Theoretical questions place a person in a hypothetical situation. (For example, 'How would you run a client event?') This style of questioning is not used much today as it tests a candidate's ability to answer a question, rather than how they might perform. Use this style of question only if the candidate has no experience.

Behavioural questions are the questions you need to ask. They seek demonstrated examples of behaviours from a candidate's past experience and concentrate on job-related competencies and behaviours. These questions ask for real-life examples. (For example, 'Tell me about a recent experience where you were required to handle a difficult customer complaint.')

Leading questions hint at the answer the interviewer is seeking and should be avoided. (For example, 'Working on your own doesn't concern you, does it?') *Many* interviewers unconsciously fall back on this style of questioning, so watch out for it—you'll be surprised how often you do this. You will also tend to do it more when you are interviewing a candidate you start to get excited about and to believe is right for the job.

Open questions look for detail or more information on a subject. They often start with words such as 'Describe how you ...' or 'Tell me more about ...'.

Step 3: Conduct the interview — the STAR technique

When conducting the interview, assess the candidate's answer using the best practice STAR technique.

> The STAR technique helps you to identify what actually happened in a given situation, the timing (when did it actually happen?), the action they took and the result. In short:
>
> Situation — a brief overview of what happened
>
> Time — when did this happen?
>
> Action — what specific action did they take?
>
> Result — was there a positive result or outcome?

Your candidates won't know to answer in this specific way, but it is your role to draw out the information you need to make an informed decision.

Step 4: Rank responses

To maintain objectivity you must use a uniform approach to evaluating all candidates. This is particularly important when conducting a panel interview.

First, the roles and responsibilities of the position should be broken down into the various skills required to perform them. The next step is to rank the candidate's competency in each of these skills, for example as A ('Demonstrated'), B ('Partially demonstrated') or C ('Not demonstrated').

These rankings could be further defined as follows.

Demonstrated. The candidate shows a solid knowledge and experience in the skill. They could be expected to perform it autonomously as part of their role and would be able to train/supervise others in this skill, if required.

Partially demonstrated. The candidate understands and is able to demonstrate the skill. They could be expected to perform it autonomously as part of their role, but further training may be required at a later stage to hone their skills.

Not demonstrated. The candidate has little or no understanding/experience in the required skill. They would need supervision in this area before being allowed to work autonomously. Training in the skill should be given as part of the candidate's induction.

Table 13.1 shows an example of how you can apply this approach.

Table 13.1: assessing the candidate's competencies

	Competency 1 Teamwork	Competency 2 Planning	Competency 3 Writing skills
Candidate 1	A	C	B
	Evidence:	Evidence:	Evidence:
Candidate 2	B	B	C
	Evidence:	Evidence:	Evidence:

Using this method, each interviewer can quickly and easily register their estimate of competency for each skill. The rankings can then be discussed in detail following the interview to gauge if the candidate should progress to the next stage of the interview.

Step 5: Evaluate results

Compare objective measures by evaluating the results across all candidates and then comparing these to the job requirements.

If you conducted a panel interview, compare your scores with those of other interviewers. Discuss overall evidence and findings, and explore any differences in opinion to decide who proceeds to the next stage.

Finally, inform all candidates of the results, not just the ones who make it! It is important that you manage this process well, as how you treat people will get out into the market and can affect your reputation and brand. Remember, you are managing perceptions right through the process until the day the new person starts.

The period between making an offer and the start date is also a highly critical time. Ensure you maintain contact with the successful candidate through the period of their resignation and transfer. It is a good way to shape positive perceptions in your new team member. Invitations to team meetings, conferences or social events will be appreciated. It is about setting up a success pathway for every person who starts.

Chapter summary

- The first key to managing performance is to make sure you recruit the right people with the right skills and the *right mindset* in the first place.

- Conduct a behavioural interview so the focus is on fact rather than hypothesis.

- A behavioural interview consists of these elements:

  ➤ analyse the job

  ➤ develop structured questions

  ➤ conduct the interview

  ➤ rank responses

  ➤ evaluate results.

- Decide if the interview is the only selection method you will use or if any other evaluation methodologies would be appropriate.

- Be aware that where you conduct the interview will send a clear message about your organisation.

- When evaluating a candidate's competency in each skill required for the role, the process will be faster if a uniform ranking system is used by each person on the interview panel.

- Ensure that the interview process is managed professionally, as how you treat people will get out into the market and can affect your reputation and brand.

- Maintain contact with the successful candidate through the period of their resignation. It is a good way to shape positive perceptions in your new team member.

- In a candidate's answer, look for:

  ➤ Situation (a brief overview)

  ➤ Time (when it happened)

- ➤ Action (what specific action they took)
- ➤ Result (any positive result or outcome).

- Once it is decided who is proceeding to the next stage, inform *all* candidates, not just the successful ones.

Reflective questions

1. Think about three people who left your team and organisation in the past year. Why do you think they left?

2. Was there anything you could have done during the recruitment process that could have prevented their leaving?

3. Think about the last time you interviewed someone for a role. How much time (in minutes) did you spend preparing for the interview?

4. What emphasis did you put on reviewing all paperwork before the interview?

5. How much time did you spend going through the job description?

6. How much time did you spend re-evaluating the advert to see if there was anything you could have missed when writing it or asking others to write it?

7. How did you *objectively* evaluate the quality of the candidate's answers?

8. How did you let every candidate know whether they were successful or not?

9. Could you have improved how you did this?

10. How did you actively stay in touch with the successful recruit between offering them the job and their start date?

Where to start

1. Consider the list of questions you will ask the next time you interview someone to ensure you improve the likelihood of a successful hire.

2. Draw up an evaluation methodology that ensures as much objectivity as possible.

3. Write down the STAR technique and prompt for answers that fulfil the criteria.

4. Draw up a plan to ensure you maintain frequent contact between offering the job and the new recruit's start date. This is particularly important, for reasons you will discover in the next chapter.

chapter 14

The 90-day critical period—how to attach and align your people

Once your new employee is on board they will start to follow a pathway where the aim should be to achieve competence in their role as soon as possible. In most organisations this takes approximately three months or 90 days. This period is often referred to as the 90-day critical period.

During this time it is critical that your new team member bonds, connects or attaches to the organisation, their role and their line manager.

This *attachment phase* actually starts *before* the new employee has joined your organisation or team, as illustrated in figure 14.1 (overleaf).

Figure 14.1: the attachment phase

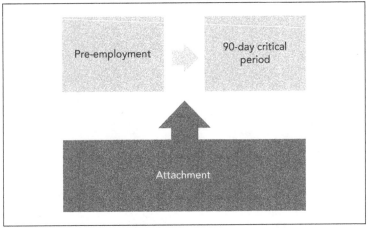

Before we look at each of the stages to attaching a new team member, let's be clear on what attachment and alignment actually mean.

Attachment and alignment

Attachment occurs on three levels:

1. *Attachment to the organisation.* The top six factors that attach an employee to an organisation are values, mission, industry, culture, success, and learning and development program.

2. *Attachment to the role.* The top six factors that attach an employee to their role are: status or level of the role; money; tasks and activities associated with the role; positioning of the role within the organisation; learning, development and growth opportunities; and future prospects.

3. *Attachment to the line manager.* The top six factors that attach an employee to a manager are character, attitude, capability, leadership and management skills, knowledge and mentor/coaching skills.

Equally important, and often overlooked, however, is *alignment*.

Alignment means all parties are on the same page and agree on expectations. When this occurs you achieve *positive attachment*.

Negative attachment, on the other hand, means only one factor is in play—that is, a party is either 'aligned but not attached' or 'attached but not aligned'.

For example, a person in your team is attached to the role because it satisfies their need for status, money and job content; but they are not aligned or in agreement with your requirements and expectations of the role. Or a team member may be aligned in terms of expectations of the role but not attached or bonded to either you or the organisation. When this is the case you know you will not be able to achieve high performance, let alone sustain it.

Now we understand attachment and alignment, let's look at the two phases in which they occur: the pre-employment phase and the 90-day critical period.

The pre-employment phase

The pre-employment phase begins when a future team member comes on the radar of the organisation through a job ad, web search or referral.

During this stage your goal is to ensure that the potential future team member has a positive and professional experience with you and the organisation, as discussed in the previous chapter, and that you are both aligned in terms of expectations.

These expectations relate to the role, the organisation, expected behaviours, management and so on. One of the key areas where people fall down is that the expectations are not clear or are misrepresented on some level by one or both parties. The methodology outlined in chapter 13 will minimise this risk.

> In summary, the things that really count during the pre-employment phase are:
>
> - job representation
> - process and timing
> - understanding the vision, mission and values
> - high-level communications before and after the job offer
> - individual and organisational values alignment.

Once the employee joins your team and organisation they enter the second phase of *attachment and alignment*.

The 90-day critical period

The 90-day critical period must be understood by every manager. What happens during this phase will critically impact the engagement and retention of the new employee. It shapes the thought processes and mindset of the employee. The expression 'First impressions count' is no understatement.

This is the most impressionable stage for a new employee. They are sensitive to everything going on around them. If things do not go well you may struggle to undo any negative impressions and behaviours formed at this stage. What a new employee notices, consciously or subconsciously, will shape their perceptions and provide their 'moments of truth' about how things are done within the organisation.

During this time you, as their manager, will again be under intense scrutiny. The employee will be evaluating whether what you said to them during the interview process about both the role and the organisation is true, just as you will be gauging whether their skills in fact match their claims.

When an employee is not 100 per cent confident (few employees are at this stage, as they are still learning processes and routines), they rely particularly on observation—evaluating safety threats and looking for endorsement and attention from you while they gain the confidence to work autonomously.

So what are the key things to focus on in the first 90 days? This is where the psychological contract starts to really come into play. We discussed this idea in detail in the introduction, but let's remind ourselves of the core components.

A *psychological* contract is concerned with intentions and expectations between parties. It is an informal agreement that is typically based on people's perceptions. These perceptions relate to notions of give and take between two individuals, what is right and wrong, how people should work together, what is and is not fair, and loyalty and trust.

The employment contract — a seven-point reminder

- The psychological contract is far more powerful than the employment contract.

- The employment contract will not unlock potential and high performance, whereas the psychological will do exactly this because it is based on *thoughts, feelings* and *emotions*.

- The psychological contract goes both ways and is based on very significant human behaviours and values that, for many, will either help build a relationship or break it in an instant. These include fairness, loyalty, respect and trust.

(continued)

The employment contract — a seven-point reminder (cont'd)

- Managers must accept that reality is *not* enough; it must be demonstrated to and perceived by your people.

- Managers must understand the perceptions their team have of them in terms of their obligations to the team, their personal behaviour, how they deal with staff and others, and the quality of their work.

- When the contract is broken, typically it has nothing to do with tasks, competence, technology, policies, practices, procedures or products. It occurs when the people factors are overlooked.

- Typically, it begins with a sense of discomfort, which starts to grow, reducing resilience and leading to varying degrees of disengagement and disconnection. Left unchecked, it can escalate to passive or active withdrawal, acts of aggression or even sabotage such as petty theft, and the formation of team alliances that undermine the manager or organisation.

Another process that has a big impact on the psychological contract is induction.

Induction

Most organisations still don't understand the five stages of a best practice induction process: orientation, core messages, rotation, incremental learning and end of induction/ probation feedback (see figure 14.2).

Figure 14.2: the five stages of a best practice induction process

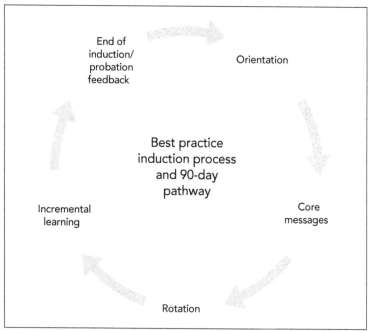

If your organisation does not commit to this process, then as a manager you must find a way to carry it through yourself, as it will serve you very well in the long run. The induction stage is critical to ensuring:

1. employee bonding and establishment of the terms of the psychological contract

2. the achievement of minimum competency in the shortest time frame

3. the employee's perception of self-worth and contribution to team

4. an accurate determination of a new employee's likely success.

Let's take a look at the objectives for each phase.

Orientation phase

During this part of the 90-day critical period, a new team member is coming to grips with an overload of information and trying to sort out and retain the key elements. An orientation session typically includes: meet-and-greets with fellow team members, management and colleagues from other departments; familiarisation with their physical work environment and the layout of the building itself; and a chance to get settled in their work space.

Core messages

During this stage a new team member should be reminded of the key focus for them and the company. It typically includes: an introduction to the company and its history; clarification of the company's mission statement or central vision; a briefing by the CEO explaining the 'why' of the company; and information on communication practices and the culture of the company the ('how things are done around here'), including expectations of behaviours and protocols.

Rotation

During this stage the new team member will have an opportunity to see their team or department in action. The rotation session typically includes: an opportunity to sit in with team members and observe the process; a 'big picture' briefing on how their work fits into the entire company process; and an opportunity to sit in with other department team members to observe the process and impact of their work and to see first-hand how other departments will rely on them.

Incremental learning

While the information conveyed during the 90-critical period is essential for a new team member to be able to attach and align with a company, the rate at which the information is communicated needs to be monitored so it is not only understood but also retained.

Typically, this learning should take place over the three months—*not* in a one-week download, as occurs in many organisations.

Make a checklist of all the relevant processes to be learned and where possible allocate these across the team, choosing those who have the best skills in any particular area. This way the workload is shared, the work is spread out appropriately over time and your team members get to know each other. This way the whole team have a role in supporting the new member, and attachment and bonding are encouraged.

End of induction / probation feedback

Typically the end of the best practice induction process coincides with the end of the probation feedback and review session. During this session your goal is to ensure your team member is competent in their role at a basic level. If they are not, this process should be used to establish goals for how both you as the manager and the team member plan to get there.

This is your opportunity to honestly review whether *you* have done everything possible and necessary to help your team member achieve competence. If you have, then now is the time to provide absolute clarity about what must be achieved, and by when, in order for the new team member to stay with the organisation—and succeed.

In summary, the attachment and alignment phase serves to prepare the new employee for success by addressing those areas that will have the biggest impact on their mindset. These include:

- vision, mission and values
- leadership and management trust, credibility and relationships
- care and value of employees as an individual not as commodities
- demonstrated support of and for your people
- communication practices between departments, suppliers, customers, peers and managers
- culture ('how things are done around here')
- coaching and mentoring support and guidance
- peer and stakeholder interaction
- work environment
- policies and procedures
- resources
- explanation of their duties and requirements
- scope of responsibility
- who they will report to formally and informally
- their targets
- performance review systems
- learning and development opportunities.

There are 10 core areas, called the 90-day attachment and alignment drivers.They also contribute greatly to the strength of the psychological contract between the organisation, the manager and the new team member. All of these drivers work together to ensure that at the 90-day mark the employee will be competent in their role, have established good relationships, understand policies and procedures, and know where to go for additional information.

The Core 90-Day Drivers

- Recruitment process

- Induction process

- Role expectations

- Coach and mentor support

- Management and leadership

- Peer and stakeholder interaction

- Culture and values

- Work environment

- Policies and procedures

- Resources available.

HCM Global and Career Crowd® conduct 90-day Performance Alignment Surveys to collect feedback from both managers and employees on how their first three months went overall, to identify differences in perceptions and to find how their experience could be improved. They also provide us with feedback on the strength of the psychological contract and the level of attachment achieved at this stage.

It is important to note that this is all done *before* the probation period is completed to ensure fairness and reduce subjectivity in the process.

Typically, the top three areas needing improvement relate to lack of support, lack of communication and lack of management. Again, you can see that these all relate to people, management and relationships—not policies, procedures and technical issues—so the good news is that the line manager can make a significant impact on controlling these issues and perceptions.

Chapter summary

■ To be a high performer, a new team member needs to attach and align with the organisation, their role and their line manager within the first 90 days.

■ For alignment to happen you must ensure expectations are clear and understood by both parties. When this occurs you achieve *positive attachment*.

■ Alignment and attachment, while linked, operate independently. Don't assume that if a new team member has one, they automatically have the other as well.

■ During both the interview and the first 90 days, your goal is to ensure that the new team member has a positive and professional experience with you and the organisation.

■ Your goals for the end of the 90-day period are for the employee to be competent in their role, to have established good relationships with you and their team, to understand policies and procedures, and to know where to go for additional information.

■ What a new employee notices, consciously or subconsciously, in their first 90 days will shape their perceptions and provide their 'moments of truth' about how things are done within the organisation.

■ Be aware that both parties will be evaluating the other during the 90-day period. The employee will be deciding if what you told them during the interview about the role and the organisation is true, just as you will be gauging whether their skills in fact match their claims. This is part of the psychological contract.

■ Your induction of the team member should include: orientation, core messages, rotation, incremental learning and end of induction/probation feedback. If your organisation does not include this process, then as a manager, you must find a way to carry it through yourself.

■ Check the feedback you received from the new team member at the end of the induction to review whether *you* have done everything possible and necessary to help the new team member achieve competence.

■ Typically, the top three areas in employee induction needing improvement relate to people (lack of support, communication and management), rather than policies, procedures or technical issues. Understand that, as the manager, you have the prime impact on controlling these issues and obtaining the desired result.

Reflective questions

1. Out of 10, rate your level of attachment to your role. Provide examples.

2. Out of 10, rate your level of attachment to your organisation. Provide examples.

3. Out of 10, rate your level of attachment to your line manager. Why is this the case?

4. Evaluate your performance as a manager during a new recruit's first 90 days.

5. How would you rate your level of direct communication with this new team member?

6. How have you actively demonstrated fairness to your new team member during their first 90 days?

7. How do you think the new team member would rate their experience so far with the organisation?

8. How do you think the new team member would rate their experience so far with you?

9. How do you think the new team member would rate their experience so far with other team members?

10. How well do you manage the end-of-probation period?

Where to start

1. Write down a list of the people in your team and evaluate (out of 10) how attached or bonded you think they are to you. From this information deduce why this is the case and how you could improve it.

2. Evaluate the induction process in your organisation and identify what you need to do to ensure all stages of best practice induction are covered, so you give a fair start to all new team members who join you.

3. Evaluate the three weakest attachment and alignment drivers during the 90-day critical period and form a plan to overcome these deficiencies.

4. Evaluate the level of alignment of each person in your team to the organisation and to their role. Identify where misalignment occurs and potential reasons why.

In each case you could engage and seek advice from your HR manager on how you might close the gaps and how they could help you do so.

chapter 15

How to increase focus and accountability

As a manager, maintaining the accountability and focus of your team should be a top priority. Make no mistake, how you do this will determine your team's level of success—and yours. It will also directly impact whether or not people consider you to be an *accountable* and *focused manager*.

Accountable managers with focused minds consistently outperform others. Having absolute clarity about what needs to be achieved and a commitment to the tasks typically gets the job done.

Managers with higher levels of control (not to be mistaken for micro-management, which is quite different) usually have greater *self*-control and focus, stay composed and positive even in testing situations, think clearly under pressure, and anticipate problems, pressure and bottlenecks.

Remember, when control is lost, fear rises and emotions are triggered, undermining stability in performance and relationships.

Let's start with accountability.

As a manager you must ensure you build an accountable team, and to do this you must provide absolute clarity around your expectations. If people know what is expected of them in terms of tasks and time frames, then they know what they need to deliver and by when.

Setting the right expectations

Do this well early on and it is guaranteed to save you much emotional energy and time down the track. In our experience, most negative feedback conversations link back to the original expectations of an employee and are due to a lack of clarity up front or unrealistic expectations. This is why when setting expectations they need to be the *right* expectations. For example, I know many ineffective managers who are very clear on what they expect, but their expectations are not realistic, which means they are setting up the team member to become daunted, fearful or paralysed from the outset.

So the first step is to qualify and validate your expectations, adopting the right mindset and using objective data, not basing your expectations on hopes, ideals and unfair comparisons. You are then ready to conduct the conversation using as your pathway the TALKING Process model introduced in chapter 8.

Remember, the TALKING model is designed to help you to plan and execute a challenging conversation, to build rapport and reinforce mutual respect, to reinforce mutual purpose, to ensure the conversation is as objective as possible, and to reveal and test assumptions and perceptions.

The great thing about this conversation is that it is the least challenging management conversation you can have, as it is totally expected and, for some, even eagerly anticipated. This is an opportunity for the new team member to understand exactly what you need and expect from them, and it will serve to give them a certain level of comfort—even if your expectations are high! There is nothing worse than not knowing what is expected of you and all the time second-guessing whether or not you are on the right track.

This is probably the only performance-based conversation you will have with minimal emotion. The new recruit will be at the beginning of their journey and will be relaxed about this type of conversation.

This is also one of your very few conversations as a manager in which you will feel that *your needs* are being listened to and taken into account. Most other management conversations will feel like they're about you meeting all the different needs of your people and trying to understand what is going on with *them*. So don't miss out on this golden opportunity!

The purpose of the conversation is to set the *right* expectations in the four key areas of job role expectations, performance expectations, team expectations and organisational expectations.

Job role expectations

Too many new recruits and managers put the job description away once the induction stage is completed. Start the conversation by going through the job description in detail and filling in any blanks. Remember, the last time your new recruit probably looked at the job description in detail was before their interview, so there are likely to be questions they did not ask for fear of compromising your perception of them at the time. Check if this is the case by running through the job description and confirming with them that they understand how it all fits together.

This is not a one-off exercise either. As their manager, you should check in on the job description at all goal-setting and performance stages, such as at the end of their probation period, at their first six-month review and at their end-of-year performance review.

Performance expectations

You must be able to articulate what the key performance indicators are for the role. Most organisations have these formalised for each role. If your company does not, then this is *your job.*

You must be able to articulate your expectations and how you are going to assess whether or not they are being achieved. This usually means some kind of measurement is involved, whether in terms of numbers of something being done or completed, deadlines achieved or client satisfaction rates, for example.

As a manager you must be able to 'measure' everything done in your team; there is no other way to calculate *objectively* what is being achieved. If you don't have these numbers and facts, then you will be entering dangerous waters where measurements are based on perceptions rather than proof—and this is when the really tricky conversations occur.

Team expectations

Now is also a great opportunity to share how the team works and functions. Begin by discussing how each role impacts the other roles in the team and what the ramifications are if the work is not done in line with team expectations. One way to achieve this is first to explain the role dynamics and then to ensure your new recruit sits with all other team members as part of their induction and orientation process. This will serve to give the new recruit both a first-hand appreciation of how the roles interrelate and one-on-one work bonding time with their new team mates.

Organisation expectations

Finally, organisation expectations should be discussed during the new recruit's induction program. If your organisation does not have a formal induction program, again it is your job to see to this. To attach your new recruit to the goals of the organisation, you must share big-picture information and map out for them how their role plays a vital part in the pursuit of much broader goals.

Expectations of the team member

Points to cover include noting their expectations and addressing any questions or concerns, for example about avenues for advancement, options for up-skilling, remuneration, their co-workers, work activities and employee benefits.

It's all about setting a climate that places a high value on competence, loyalty, trust and alignment. This is what people need in order to perform at beyond minimal competence levels, volunteering discretional effort.

Once expectations have been set, and understood by both team member and manager, it's time to focus your attention on tasks essential to running a high performance team.

So now your team members are absolutely clear on what needs to be delivered, and by when, your next job is to keep your team focused so that they don't take their eye off the ball and keep on track at all times.

Typically, when expectations are not met it comes down to a lack of focus in four key areas: planning and control, meetings, emails or procrastination.

Planning and control

Failing to plan means planning to fail. Without careful planning and control, you will not achieve sustained high performance.

High performance comes from thoroughly laid plans, anticipation and laser focus. Your aim should be to prepare and guide your team to face each day in a proactive rather than reactive way. An ideal mix is for the team to be in proactive mode for at least 80 per cent of the day, allowing up to 20 per cent of time for any unexpected or urgent demands. By contrast, underperforming teams tend to spend 80 per cent of their time in reactive mode and only 20 per cent on proactive work. Worse still, these teams often will not accept that there is another way of working and are convinced they work harder than anyone else and they have no more time to give.

Through the course of my career I have watched people move from organisation to organisation and with each move gain a different perspective on what it means to 'work hard'. I constantly have to explain that everyone works hard these days and it is not a phenomenon that is particular to any one organisation. Most people look at me in disbelief!

I have seen people work at what they believe is their absolute capacity, without a minute to spare, only to move to another organisation where their productivity and work capacity increases massively. Then, after an adjustment period and good management, a new norm is set.

Many people are capable of feats well beyond what they initially think is achievable. This of course comes back to mindset. As an illustration of self-limiting beliefs think about the four-minute-mile record broken by Roger Bannister in 1954. In the ensuing months a number of other runners also broke through this barrier, which was previously deemed unassailable.

The first step in planning and control is focused goal setting.

Focused goal setting

This means gaining absolute clarity about what has to be achieved and by when. One of the best tools for this purpose is the SMART goals model, a widely used best practice model to help managers focus their people on *outcomes* and *performance*.

SMART is an acronym for:

Specific

Measurable

Achievable

Relevant

Timely.

Step 1: Specific

Clearly state *exactly* what has to be achieved. Think about what the task actually involves. For example, rather than something like 'Improve communications with the manufacturing department', describe in as much detail as possible specifically what needs to be achieved, such as:

> Create a systems process for the team so that all requests for information or materials from the manufacturing department are fully processed and sent within 24 hours. To be completed by 30 June.

Step 2: Measurable

You must be able to 'measure' every goal you set. Consider what is to be achieved. Add a number or time frame into the goal: how much, how many or what percentage.

Step 3: Achievable

Establish that every goal you set can be realistically achieved by your people. Consult with your team to ensure you are being fair and reasonable in what you are asking of them.

Step 4: Relevant

What are the reasons behind choosing these goals? Is this the best timing and use of resources? Are the goals relevant to the business requirements or performance required of your people?

Step 5: Timely

Set a realistic time frame for the completion of the goal. It can always be revised if there are unforeseen issues. Once you have set a time frame, communicate it to those involved. Request their feedback and secure their commitment to meeting the deadline.

Note that the TALKING Process model can be used here for this conversation. The issue this time becomes the goal-setting element.

Focused planning and prioritisation

So your people know your expectations and the goals are set. it's now your job to help your team plan and prioritise on a daily, weekly, monthly, quarterly and annual basis to maintain focus.

The team should have a good sense of what they are here to do and achieve every day. To support these goals, have them join you in implementing this five-step planning schedule every morning.

The five-step planning schedule

1. Review yesterday and ask myself, 'How did I go? Did I get through everything?'

2. Review my work for today, tomorrow and the week ahead. What do I need to do?

3. Check appointments and meetings. What do I need to prepare ahead of time?

4. Review my to-do list.

5. Prioritise each task on the list.

In carrying out these steps, you and they will get a very real sense of what is happening and, more importantly, what is on the horizon. Often, knowing what is coming up is all the motivation your people need to get through their tasks today, tomorrow or this week.

Too often, team members don't do this because they fear what is around the corner. Their mindset is that they 'will deal with it when it happens' or they 'don't have time to plan'.

The to-do list is an essential business document. Your team cannot be effective unless everyone keeps their own list up to date. Most people will say they have one, but to be truly effective it needs a certain structure. It's not just a bunch of random entries on a notepad, sticky notes or whiteboard.

As a minimum, a to-do list must have four columns—for the task name, due date, time to complete and some form of prioritisation code, such as (A) Critical—must be done today; (B) Important—should be done today; and (C) Less important—to be completed once all the more important tasks are completed.

This level of definition makes it clear both to you and to the staff member how things are going. Using this system, you will start to get a sense of what issues could arise that might affect you and your team in the coming days or weeks. The time estimate gets people thinking and calculating how long tasks will take. Doing this regularly will help you and them understand where their time is going and will ultimately drive greater efficiency.

As a manager, you must be aware of what is going on, what tasks are being put off, where time is going and what bottlenecks are developing. Over the long term it will serve to relieve pressure on both you and your team.

There may be some initial resistance as your team adapt to this approach, but in the end they will thank you for it, as everything will be accounted for and they will gain a feeling of greater control.

Tips on prioritising

- Instigate the five-step plan across the team so every team member reviews their workload each day.

- Ensure to-do lists are kept by everyone.

- Priority coding of every item allows everyone to identify what is important and urgent.

- Do not let reactivity take up more than 20 per cent of the day.

- Use guesstimates of time required for tasks to get a sense of approaching bottlenecks and plan accordingly.

Meetings are another area where time can be wasted and stress caused through a lack of focus, planning and goal setting.

Focused meetings

How you run your meetings is critical to creating awareness in others of how you do business and what you expect. Remember, people want to connect with you regularly, *even if they say they don't need to*. People need to connect with others in their team too. How you run your meetings will shape how people think and feel week to week. They want to trust you to keep everything on track.

People will stay connected to those they trust to get a job done, and meetings help you persuade them of this. But there are other reasons why you should hold a meeting. Consider the following questions to help you determine whether it's time to meet:

• Do you require information, input or advice from your team?

• Do you need your team to participate in making a decision or solving a problem?

• Do you need to share information, offer praise or give feedback?

• Do you need to hear varying perspectives on a particular issue?

• Do you need to determine or clarify responsibilities for tasks?

• Do you feel your team just needs to get together?

The focused meeting format involves the following steps.

Step 1: Focus your meeting

An agenda is the best way to ensure you achieve the aims and objectives of your meetings. More often than not, this is omitted because, ironically, people claim they 'don't have time' to put an agenda together. The outcome? Time is wasted.

Having a clear idea of what is to be achieved in a meeting is vital to its success. Your credibility as a leader rests on the perceptions your team members have of you. If you cannot run a meeting effectively, this will affect how others judge you in your role. You therefore have a clear opportunity to showcase your skills and shape the perceptions others have of you. So during the meeting your people must see you in control, being fair, delivering on your promises, holding people accountable, thinking ahead and allowing for the unexpected.

As a good leader, you will also have anticipated the likely responses of your team members to certain items ahead of time!

Use the pre-meeting preparation checklist in table 15.1 during your preparation.

Table 15.1: pre-meeting preparation checklist

Meeting details	Notes
1. The meeting's purpose	
2. The desired outcomes/objectives	
3. Meeting logistics: date, place, time, duration	
4. Who should attend?	
5. Agenda items to be covered/person responsible/time allotted	
6. How will I set expectations and allocate responsibility?	
7. Names and roles of external parties to be invited	
8. Is this a team coaching opportunity? How should I prepare?	
9. How will I motivate my team in this meeting?	
10. Pre-meeting preparation time allotted/ background material required	

Step 2: Focus responsibilities

One of the primary reasons meetings go off track is because participants do not understand their role and the expectations you have of them. Take time this week to clarify your expectations. This will help you not only improve the quality of your meetings but speed them up too!

> Three common roles and expectations for you to consider are:
>
> - *the participant*—is actively engaged by offering ideas and by helping keep the discussion on track
>
> - *the leader*—may or may not run the meeting but does clarify its purpose, its objectives and the follow-up required
>
> - *the facilitator* — guides the group through the discussion, facilitating problem solving and decision making and defusing any tension.

Step 3: Focused execution

Keeping a meeting on track is often easier said than done! Competing agendas, differing personalities and a lack of clear goals are only some of the issues that take a meeting off target.

Most often, it's the differing team personalities that derail purposeful meetings. Therefore it is important that all participants have an opportunity, and are encouraged, to share their thoughts and add input.

As a starting point, let the group know how important it is to bring up all options, concerns and issues, even if they are difficult to raise. Be sure always to thank a person if they brought up a controversial or different viewpoint. Reinforce the idea that to do this is often the key to getting the best solutions and that you (and the team) will consider all options, even if the idea is not adopted in the end.

Ensuring you spend time making it safe for everyone to be involved is vital. Listen to the dominating personalities but also make time for the quieter participants, perhaps by asking them, directly at times, what their thoughts and opinions are.

Follow the meeting guidelines checklist in figure 15.1 to help keep the meeting on track. Take it with you to your next meeting and use it to review the meeting afterwards.

Figure 15.1: meeting guidelines checklist

✓	Begin the meeting on time.
✓	Clarify agenda, objectives and outcomes required.
✓	Agree on agenda now, if not agreed beforehand.
✓	Establish the ground rules in terms of behaviours and roles.
✓	Monitor your own level of participation to make sure you are not dominating the discussion.
✓	Make it possible for shy or quiet people to contribute. Control interruptions and dominators.
✓	Be positive and encouraging about things people say.
✓	Maintain control if tensions arise.
✓	Record decisions made and action to be taken.
✓	Record input on a flipchart.
✓	End on time.

Step 4: Focused decisions

Decisions can be made 'on the go' or can be deferred. It depends on the depth of decision making required and the availability of information.

Remember, you are not solely responsible for the decision-making process. However, you are responsible for driving the process towards a desired outcome. Your preparation before the meeting is critical so you can stay one step ahead and can evaluate the quality of ideas put forward in line with or contrary to your own thinking. Always be prepared to adapt or change your ideas and keep an open mind so you are not perceived to have already made the decisions.

Recording the ideas generated during the meeting for reference during and after the meeting is very valuable. This can usually be done on a whiteboard, flipchart or some other form of public display. Mind mapping often helps here too.

Decisions can be made by the following methods:

- *Voting by majority.* This can be your fastest option. However, it may require people to take a public stand on an issue, which may put them in a win/lose situation, so be careful!

- *Group consensus.* This means reaching a decision that everyone understands, can support and is willing to help implement. Individual members may still feel that other options are preferable, but genuine consensus rallies all members behind a decision.

- *Leader's decision.* This option is most effective when there is little time to reach a decision (perhaps in a crisis) without adverse impact, and when all members understand why the leader is making the decision. But be sure to demonstrate you have considered all opinions and gained input from your team.

Having reached agreement it's time to formally wrap up the meeting. Use the end-of-meeting checklist in table 15.2 (overleaf).

Table 15.2: end-of-meeting checklist

Items to be covered	Notes
1. Check agenda—have you covered everything?	
2. Review and summarise what has been achieved.	
3. Clarify action items and deadlines.	
4. Schedule next meeting.	
5. Seek feedback from the team to help evaluate the success of the meeting.	
6. Thank participants.	

Step 5: Focused follow-up

This is usually the part of the meeting process that fails. If your expectations are not clear before, during and after the meeting, its likelihood of success is greatly reduced.

Consistency is the key to successful meetings. A consistent approach on your part ensures a consistent approach from your team! So at the end of the meeting be sure to agree on and document responsibilities, accountability and deadlines.

The next step is to fix a date to follow up via email or phone or face to face, and then '*just do it*'! Remember, your follow-up actions set the tone for the future behaviour required!

Focused email control

For all its advantages, email has the potential to seriously undermine the performance of your team and get out of control. As a manager you must ensure your team are on top of their emails and have a good system in place to deal with them.

For example, the number of emails someone has in their inbox gives a sense of the level of control they have over their work. This number will typically range between 100 and over 5000. Rarely do you find someone who can view all of their emails on one screen without having to scroll down and down and down. This is loss of control! Your people must know exactly what is in their inbox, what needs to be dealt with and who is waiting on what. With screens and screens of emails, it is only a matter of time before someone will be let down or a deadline missed.

To work towards regaining control, have your people 'chunk' their time and focus on dealing with batches of emails at certain times of the day. This allows them to put some concentrated head time into their other priorities. Most clients can wait a certain time for a response. Your team will not be efficient if they read every email as it arrives. This is 'busyness' but it is not efficient or effective.

Remind the team that their emails should serve as a virtual to-do list; the only emails that should sit in their inbox for more than three days or so are those on which action is required. All other emails should be read, filed, deleted or archived.

Help your people get on top by sitting with them and clearing their inboxes. They will be frightened at first that you are going to permanently get rid of what they might need later. This is easily overcome by company archiving processes or by your setting up an 'archive' file for them in their inbox—just like any other file—and dragging all emails older than three months into it. I guarantee you they will not be looking back through emails from three months ago, wondering if there was any action they did not get to and could possibly do now! Their mindset will be, 'If I haven't heard anything till now, then it's sorted'.

Mental clutter and the lack of a system to control a build-up of emails causes stress. The first step is for everyone in the team to stop email hoarding. Once they have done this, set a time frame for them to get on top of all remaining emails.

As each team member does this, and the weight of their email backlog is lifted from them, they will feel more able to deal with their role. With a greater focus on their work, you should see an increase in productivity and should have more time available to manage your own workload.

Email tips

- Hold a team email filing afternoon, when you get people to clear their inboxes and get their communications up to date.

- Help your team set up 'rules' for incoming emails so they are directed to appropriate folders for later reading. Emails from newsletters, networks and industry associations, for example, should all go to these folders rather than cluttering up their inbox.

- Put a stop to chain emails! Make a rule that if an email on a subject has gone back and forth more than four times, it's time to meet.

- At your next team meeting establish a team email policy, setting up standards and guidelines as a team. If you do it as a team and share ideas, you will likely get more buy-in.

- Discourage people from sending emails after hours! This is intrusive and a driver of much stress and anxiety within teams. When work finishes, so should the emails.

End procrastination

When it comes to performance, there are some very common mindsets that often need to be changed or adjusted (see figure 15.2). The first is that people believe they 'work better under pressure'. This is a fallacy. To get the best result, you need time to think, process and reflect. What people who like to 'perform under pressure' are really saying is that they need the deadline to get motivated.

Another mindset that sabotages focus and performance is 'The more you do, the more productive you are'. Every day we meet people who are extremely busy but are totally ineffective. They are busy being busy—in effect, filling in time.

Figure 15.2: three common procrastination mindsets

The adrenaline junkies	…wait until the last minute for the adrenaline rush because they believe they work better under pressure. These people are quite often overconfident.
The fearful	…fear failure and what others might think of them. These people typically would rather have people think they lack effort than ability. They quite often lack confidence.
The avoiders	…avoid decisions and therefore responsibility for results or outcomes. These people quite often lack motivation.

C. Northcote Parkinson famously said, 'Work expands so as to fill the time available for its completion'. Since first encountering it in management school I have never forgotten this quotation, and I see it at play time and time again. Parkinson's Law argues that people will subconsciously fill the time available for any work task.

Let's use as an example Joe, a software engineer we worked with to help restructure and reprioritise his work. After sitting with him at his desk for a few hours, we gave him a set of tasks to complete to get on top of his work and asked him to estimate how long the work would take. He calculated four hours. We then told him that on this one occasion, he needed to stay until the tasks were completed, so he could start tomorrow knowing he was on top of everything. He agreed reluctantly, as he had a social gathering that night.

'Magically', he finished all his tasks by 6 pm so he still made it!

The factors at play here were predominantly motivational:

- Tasks were confined to a set time.

- Motivation 1: There was a time goal.

- Motivation 2: There was a specific reason to finish.

- Motivation 3: He was aware of what needed to be achieved.

- Motivation 4: He had a desire to return tomorrow feeling less daunted.

Think about this with your own team. Who are your best time managers? Who are your worst? Are there motivational factors at play, both positive and negative? What category do you and your team members fall into?

Here are some tested strategies that can be used to overcome procrastination.

- Do it first and get it over with!

- Stop being afraid. It rarely turns out to be as hard as you expected.

- Schedule the job before it becomes a top priority, putting even more pressure on you.

- Get all the information you need to complete the job before you start. This will help build your confidence.

- Just do it! Often, once you have started you will wonder why you put it off in the first place.

Chapter summary

- People with focused minds are able to:
  - ➤ manage their impulsive feelings and emotions
  - ➤ stay composed and positive even in testing situations
  - ➤ think clearly and stay focused under pressure.

- Aim for your team to be in proactive mode for at least 80 per cent of the day, with an allowance of up to 20 per cent of time for any unexpected or urgent demands.

- Help your team to focus on outcomes and performance using the SMART goals model.

- As a manager, help your team plan and prioritise on a daily, weekly, monthly, quarterly and annual basis to maintain focus.

- Have your team include an estimation of time needed to do each task on their to-do list. Get them thinking and calculating how long tasks will take, as this will help you and them understand where their time is going and will ultimately drive efficiency.

- Be aware of what is going on, what tasks are being put off, where time is going and what bottlenecks are coming up. This will serve to relieve pressure on both you and your team.

- The way you run your meetings is critical to creating awareness in others of *how* you do business and what you expect. This will also fuel how people think and feel from week to week. They want to trust you to keep everything on track.

- During meetings your people must see you in control, being fair, delivering on your promises, holding people accountable, thinking ahead and dealing with the unexpected.

- For all its advantages, email has the potential to seriously undermine the performance of your team and get out of control. As a manager, you must ensure your team are on top of their emails and have a good system in place for dealing with them.

- There are three common procrastination mindsets — the Adrenaline Junkies, who think they work better under pressure and at the last minute; the Fearful, who fear failure; and the Avoiders, who do not want to take responsibility for their decisions.

Reflective questions

1. Think about your last performance review and about whether there was any evidence in there to suggest you lacked focus.

2. Was there any evidence to suggest that you might demonstrate a lack of accountability?

3. Out of 10, how would you rate yourself for clearly articulating your expectations to your team? Provide examples.

4. Does your manager think that you run a focused and accountable team?

5. How much time does your team spend putting out fires? Why do you think this? Provide examples.

6. Out of 10, evaluate the quality of your meetings in terms of outcomes.

7. How can you improve your meetings?

8. What evidence is there to suggest that your team are on top of their emails?

9. How do you handle procrastination in yourself?

10. How do you handle procrastination in your team?

Where to start

1. Get the right foundations in place from the outset. This means setting clear expectations. Do this right and less work will be needed from you to maintain the focus of your team over the long term.

2. Re-evaluate your meeting protocols. Share with your team what is not working for you and how you think things can be improved. Ask them for their feedback on how they think the meetings can be improved. You will be surprised at what they will tell you that will help you improve the format and reduce the time spent in meetings.

3. Schedule a team email archiving session. Do it together so you can motivate those who find this difficult—sit beside them to help them through it!

4. Identify the procrastinators in your team and work out why they are procrastinating. Then catch up with them and either help them to prioritise the tasks more appropriately or build their confidence in completing the task by either coaching them or helping them get started.

chapter 16

How to conduct a best practice performance review

Although this is the final chapter of the book, it is probably the most important.

I started the book by introducing and defining the role of the psychological contract and the impact it has on relationships and results. Conducting a performance review is probably the management task most likely either to strengthen the psychological contract or to break it in an instant, as both relationships and results are at play. To make things even trickier, perceptions of fairness and trust, give and take, underlie the performance review and are also key components of the psychological contract.

So what must a manager do to ensure they put their best foot forward and minimise any risk of the review becoming tricky or uncomfortable? The answer, as always, comes down to the right mindset!

The performance review mindset requires careful planning, focused execution and, as always when dealing with people, anticipation of how things are likely to play out. Typically, we find most managers will fail in one of these key areas and so perpetually find themselves in tricky situations. This results in a loss of confidence, which leads them either to avoid doing performance reviews wherever possible or to approach them in an overly aggressive way.

The key to performance reviews is to start as you mean to go on. Consistency is essential. You should train your people to anticipate how you are going to run them, what you will ask, how you will behave and the tone you will set. Remember, most people dread performance reviews as much as you do, so the best managers will work hard to reduce the fear factor—for them and for their people—and that will always come down to mindset and preparation.

So let's understand how to do this. First, we need to be clear on what the performance review is actually designed to do apart from what most people think of, which is that it is about 'giving feedback'!

The performance review actually plays an important role in building organisation capability. It is a vital component of an organisation's ability to sustain itself and to remain competitive in the future. It is also vital to determining the culture of the company in terms of communication protocols and feedback. Organisations that place a high priority on performance reviews usually have a culture of high employee engagement and high employee accountability, and an outcome focus serving to ensure results are achieved.

So this review is not a bureaucratic task about filling in paperwork for HR. It is a process that is essential to the organisation's survival. As you would expect, it is also a tool that enables management to conduct a constructive dialogue with their people around how well they have performed during any given cycle.

This chapter is designed as a guide on how to prepare, conduct and follow up on a performance review in order to have a big impact on team performance. But before we begin we need to be clear on how the performance review fits into the business's overall performance strategy.

The performance review forms part of the performance management system. Most performance management systems typically combine three key tools:

- *the performance plan*—what are we going to achieve in this cycle?

- *the training and development plan*—how are we going to acquire the skills to execute the plan?

- *the performance review meeting*—to what extent have the objectives of the plan been achieved?

The performance plan

To state the obvious, performance can only be reviewed if we know what we are reviewing! What do we mean by this? If you look at a performance review as a cycle, you will begin to understand how and when the performance plan should be utilised.

A performance plan is like a road map. It is typically written by the manager and details how the employee will go about achieving their key performance indicators (KPIs). It should document the goals, targets and projects that an employee is expected to deliver within the coming 12 months. A performance plan should be flexible so it maintains its relevance if a change is made to any role during a review cycle.

The performance plan is written at the beginning of the review cycle. Typically, organisations start their cycle at the beginning of their financial year and base it on a 12-month period. Keep this in mind when working through this chapter and check with your human resources department if you are unclear of your particular processes.

The training and development plan

As you would expect, the training and development plan sets out how to deliver on the training and development needs of the organisation. The plan focuses on where there are skills gaps, how these gaps can be closed and the type of training required.

Usually these training gaps are identified based on the competencies required to carry out a given role, and best-in-class organisations will have absolute clarity on what competencies are required for every role in their organisation. Again, this is not just to see that the paperwork is in order, but to ensure clarity around expectations, accountability and the focused delivery of results.

There should be an organisation training plan, a department training plan and also a training plan for every person in your organisation. Remember, training does not always mean costly courses, and it can be provided in many formats at low or no cost, as outlined in chapter 10.

The performance review meeting

Apart from providing a manager with insights into how their people are performing, a formal performance review meeting allows the manager to communicate the department's goals and objectives, boosting alignment to individual performance plans. It can increase productivity by providing timely feedback to employees. It helps organisations make valid decisions with respect to training and development, promotion and workforce planning. It also provides an element of protection against lawsuits brought by employees with respect to termination or denial of promotion.

Why we should assess performance

Managers must assess performance in order to understand whether the employee is meeting the key performance indicators of their role. By assessing performance, a manager is able to:

- gauge how well an employee is performing against their performance plan and objectives

- understand any challenges an employee may be facing in achieving their KPIs

- review and adjust role requirements in order to reduce activities that do not yield a result for the department

- detect and pinpoint 'performance slippage' or incompetence

- work with their people to provide a targeted training tool that enables management to have a constructive dialogue with their people about the nature of their performance.

The role of each party in a performance review

A performance review meeting requires preparation and effort by both manager and the team member.

Both should adopt a mindset of mutual purpose and mutual respect. This shared mindset requires both parties to understand and believe in the process: *We are in this together; we are both trying to help each other understand issues around performance and results, whether positive or negative; and we are both committed to ensuring we do so in a manner that is always respectful of the other person.*

Once that mindset is in play we can move on to considering what other mindsets are required by each party.

Setting the team member's mindset

As a manager you are responsible for helping set this mindset. You must help team members understand that this is a two-way process and they have as much of a part to play in it as you do.

To help set this mindset you must ask your team members to keep a log of examples of situations during a given period that validate their perceptions of their achievements. It is not good enough for a team member to say they think they had a good quarter or year, if they cannot actually provide concrete examples to support this.

Every comment on a performance review plan should be backed up with an example. These examples also help you to conduct meaningful discussions around any challenges, difficulties or concerns they have in meeting their performance objectives.

Remember, examples help reduce the subjectivity that often triggers minor or major conflict.

Setting your mindset

As manager, you are responsible for setting a positive and constructive tone during the performance review meeting, fostering mutual respect and purpose, and encouraging open and honest dialogue throughout the review.

You must always keep a log of the employee's achievements during the performance cycle, including any examples of situations that validate your assessments of the team member's strengths and limitations in performing their role.

Ensure that the SMART goals model is included in the performance plan. Coach the employee during the performance cycle, and provide training opportunities to help them improve their performance.

No surprises — the golden rule!

If there is one thing that is sure to upset the relationship between a manager and a team member, it is a surprise — and usually not a nice one! *Never* surprise your people during the performance review. It is an opportunity to summarise the feedback given and received over the past 12 months. It is *not* the time to drop a bombshell or to share your thoughts on something that happened earlier in the year that you now want to use to validate your assessments. If the incident was significant, it should have been discussed then and not saved up for the end-of-year performance review.

This is very important for maintaining trust. If your team member is surprised by your assessment, it means you have not provided them with adequate ongoing feedback and coaching during the course of the review cycle — and this is your problem, not theirs.

By eliminating the element of surprise from a performance review, we can effectively reduce anxiety on the part of both employee and manager. We achieve this by providing regular feedback and coaching during the 12-month cycle.

Planning a performance review meeting

Planning is everything! When conducting a performance review, most of the manager's work happens before the meeting.

The manager's responsibility
The manager must take the time to:

- re-read the employee's job description and update it where required

- re-read the performance plan for the previous 12 months

- assess the employee's performance against the key performance indicators, goals, core competencies and any other relevant performance criteria

---

(continued)

Planning a performance review meeting (cont'd)

- assess whether they have provided the employee with adequate coaching, training and feedback during the performance cycle

- gather feedback from peers and customers, where appropriate

- review any documentation of their observations of the employee and other relevant data

- document specific examples to support your feedback, and remember to pay equal attention to both positive and negative feedback.

The team member's responsibility

Just as a manager needs to prepare for the review, so does the employee. The best way to ensure that your employee does so is to let them know your expectations during the performance planning phase. You can also provide them with a template to complete before their formal review.

In planning for a performance review, the employee is responsible for:

- re-reading their job description and updating it as required

- re-reading their performance plan to remind themselves of their commitments

- self-assessing against their key performance indicators, goals, core competencies and any other relevant performance criteria

- reviewing the training courses they attended and determining how these courses helped them to become more competent in their role

- compiling examples of their work (including, for example, customer feedback emails and awards).

As discussed, it is essential that the team member play an active role in the performance review in order to ensure joint accountability and engagement during the process.

At this point, if you think that you are about to enter into a challenging conversation, reviewing the TALKING Process in chapter 8 will help you mentally prepare for it. If you expect the performance review meeting to be fairly straightforward, however, prepare by addressing the following seven steps, which draw on key facets of the TALKING Framework.

Seven steps in conducting a performance review

Step 1: Setting the scene

Remember, first impressions count—and this is the moment that will decide the tone of the meeting. It's the most anxious time of the discussion for both you and the employee. Getting it right will pave the way for a constructive dialogue. Depending on the culture of your organisation, you might choose to conduct this meeting in a meeting room or in a less formal way over a coffee.

Some pointers on setting the scene:

- Start by thanking the employee for preparing for the meeting.

- Review the purpose and objectives of the meeting.

- Remind the employee that this is an opportunity for them to share anything they may not already have had a chance to speak about.

- Emphasise that the purpose of the meeting is to review their performance over the past 12 months and to talk about how it can be improved for the next 12 months.

- Let them know that it is okay for them to take notes and that you will be doing the same.

Step 2: Starting a dialogue

This is your chance to gain feedback from your team member on how they view their performance to date. Ask lots of open-ended questions to get them talking. This is also a great opportunity to determine whether the employee has understood their role in the performance review meeting.

Some pointers on starting a dialogue:

Try to get the employee to talk first by asking an open-ended question. For example:

In general, how do you think you have performed overall?

What areas of your performance are you most proud of?

Why are you most proud of these areas?

What areas do you think you could improve in?

Step 3: Providing feedback

This is your opportunity to share your feedback and observations on how the employee has performed. Keep the focus of the discussion on performance rather than on personality traits. Focus on facts and be very careful with the words you use.

Some feedback examples:

Thanks for sharing your feedback with me. It's great that you have put a lot of thought into this review, and I appreciate this.

From my perspective, I am generally pleased with your feedback. During this period I have observed...

I'm really impressed with the way you have...

I have identified a couple of improvement opportunities for you to focus on. You mentioned previously that you found it difficult to...Why do you think you had difficulty in achieving these targets?

Step 4: Building agreement

This step is often either not well executed or forgotten. Building agreement is about agreeing on what has been discussed and on the final assessments. If you fail to build agreement, you can be almost certain there will be no improvement in performance.

Some approaches to building agreement:

Now we have a good understanding of your performance, we need to make sure we're on the same page as far as the assessment is concerned.

Do you feel that the assessment accurately captures your performance during this period?

If not, do you have any other comments or feedback to share?

So, based on today's discussion, we agree that you have performed well in [name areas]. and that we will work together to improve your strengths in [name areas].

Step 5: Training and development plan

A training and development plan is an essential component of an effective performance review meeting. Without it, you can expect no improvement in performance in next year's review. The objective here is to identify specific training needs that link directly to competencies required in the role.

Now you have reached mutual agreement you can begin to map out a training and development plan for the next 12 months.

Some considerations on training and development planning:

- Identify which key skills need to be improved. Be specific.

- Consider whether the employee has received any previous training/coaching in this area. If yes, explore the reasons why the learning has not been successfully applied.

- Consider whether training is the right solution.

- If training is the solution, which program(s) could improve these results?

- Document and agree on when the training will take place and how it will be delivered.

- Document how you will provide coaching support to embed any new skills learned during the training course.

Step 6: Writing a performance plan

The next step in the process is to write a performance plan. This plan will be used for the next 12-month cycle. Be sure to include both skill-specific goals and behavioural goals.

The performance plan should be future focused and document the specific key performance indicators, competencies, goals and projects for the next 12-month cycle.

When writing the plan:

- be specific about the goals and objectives the employee should achieve

- compile SMART goals (Specific, Measurable, Attainable, Relevant, Timely)

- ensure that all performance gaps are covered.

Step 7: Record keeping and follow-up

The final step is to document in writing what has been discussed and agreed. If you have not already documented the discussion, now is the time to do so!

Summing up:

- Summarise feedback, beginning with positive comments.

- Confirm the next steps for improving performance, where applicable.

- Review the new performance plan and the new training plan.

- Before concluding the meeting, conduct a brief review. Ask the employee what was useful and not so useful about the meeting. Also ask for their suggestions about what you could do to make future feedback sessions more helpful.

- Thank the employee for their commitment.

- Provide the employee with a copy of the recorded conversation.

Final tips for giving and receiving feedback

The 7-Step Feedback Process

- Describe specifically what you are observing.

- Tell them about the direct impact of their action.

- Give the person an opportunity to explain.

- Draw out their ideas.

- Offer specific suggestions for improvement.

- Summarise and express support.

- Follow up.

Giving feedback

- Express your feedback in positive terms.

- Gather your evidence before you address an issue.

- Be alert to individual personalities and how someone may react.

- Use 'I' statements to describe how the behaviour is affecting you.

- Be descriptive rather than evaluative.

- Be specific rather than general.

- Focus on improving performance.

- Feedback should be future focused.

- One-off incidences may be better left unmentioned.

- Don't limit feedback to poor performance.

- Provide feedback as soon as possible after the behaviour.

Receiving feedback

- Listen actively.

- Manage your own response.

- If the employee becomes defensive, paraphrase them to confirm your understanding.

- Distinguish whether the giver is really trying to help you or responding out of anger.

- Paraphrase what you hear and ask questions to clarify.

- Separate fact from opinion.

- Be attentive to constructive suggestions you can act on.

Now you have delivered a best practice performance review, you and your team member are set up well for the months or year ahead!

In carrying out this process, by adopting the right mindsets I hope you will have achieved your ultimate goal as a manager and human being: knowing that you have done everything you possibly could to ensure you were fair, honest and objective, and always acted to encourage mutual respect and mutual purpose.

In fact, this approach should underlie everything you do in management.

Management is an art, not a science. There are no certainties or guarantees, because you are dealing with people!

As shown in this chapter, and indeed throughout the book, you can dramatically impact your results from TODAY. By choosing the right management mindsets, you will generate the thoughts and feelings required of our new 21st century workforce, knowing that these thoughts and feelings will either drive them to achieve more—or turn off this desire in an instant.

Everything we have talked about in *The Four Mindsets* comes together at this point.

Our starting point was to understand the psychological contract and the perceptions of give and take, fairness and trust, before we considered how our new generations think, the impact of thoughts and feelings, and the formation of mindsets.

We explored emotional intelligence and the power it has to influence others, how to connect with people at a deeper level of understanding, recognising their hot and cold buttons, even how they think, and how from this we can predict a variety of situations with great accuracy.

Continuing our journey we studied the roles of confidence—a teachable skill—and coaching and training in how people grow.

And on to our final destination, where we have the right people on board who are always focused and accountable and who, through the performance review, know exactly where they are going and how they will get there!

This pathway is tried and tested, and it does deliver results. We have turned around many teams and organisations using this methodology, transforming poor performers into the highest performing teams in organisations of up to 35 000 staff.

This success has set new industry standards and created recognised centres of excellence. At times it has been tough and our beliefs and resilience tested, but I have a few mantras that have always served me and my teams well.

The first is this:

There is always a way!

I truly believe there is no business problem for which a solution cannot be found. It's a matter of, yes, mindset—and this mindset requires determination, persistence and at times an iron will.

The second mantra was used at the Telstra Business Women of the Year Awards in 2012 to introduce me on stage. I didn't realise the full significance of it then but I do now, which is the reason I share it with you here.

I believe if you do the right things the right things happen. This means doing the hard work, constantly learning, empathising with others, and having the genuine desire to get the very best result you are capable of—both for you and for others too.

In management if you take short cuts, or fail to do what you know is the right thing, you reduce your chances of success and increase the likelihood of conflict or difficult situations.

Call it karma—the universe, or some other godly power, always knows!

If you do the right thing, though, then the right thing always happens. Ask my staff! This plays out time and time again, although sometimes you need patience!

However, even with these mantras and the best of intentions, there will be days when things don't work out, the results are not as you intended and you do not feel like you are a good manager. This is when you have to have belief in yourself and find a way to not buckle under the pressure.

I have been teaching management for 23 years now across two very different management eras. There is no doubt that today's successful managers are those who are most resilient and who operate as human beings first and managers second.

They are the people who are prepared to look first within before making assumptions and passing judgements on others. They are very competent at their jobs and are visible, but they do not require the adulation of others to get the job done.

They understand how people think and feel every day and steer their people to the realisation of their known or hidden potential—and to high performance. They seem to have the magical skill of getting the job done *and* being attentive and caring for others.

But we now know that there is actually nothing magical in this—it is simply the Four Mindsets at work.

Index

Index

 GLOBAL

career crowd™

A Multi Award Winning Learning Company

People and Performance

Conference Keynotes, Masterclasses & Workshops

Post Conference Learning Support

Four Mindsets® Licensed Training and Coaching Programs

Training Courses and Programs

Coaching Programs

Co Mentoring Groups

Webinar Learning Series

Consulting Services

Contact us at
info@hcmglobal.biz
info@fourmindsets.com
www.fourmindsets.com

Connect with us on
in Anna-Lucia Mackay
@annaluciamackay
@annaluciamackay

Connect
with WILEY ▶▶▶

WILEY

Browse and purchase the full range of Wiley publications on our official website.

www.wiley.com

Check out the Wiley blog for news, articles and information from Wiley and our authors.

www.wileybizaus.com

Join the conversation on Twitter and keep up to date on the latest news and events in business.

@WileyBizAus

Sign up for Wiley newsletters to learn about our latest publications, upcoming events and conferences, and discounts available to our customers.

www.wiley.com/email

Wiley titles are also produced in e-book formats. Available from all good retailers.

WILEY

Learn more with practical advice from our experts

Ignite
Gabrielle Dolan

Humanise
Anthony Howard

Extraordinary Leadership in Australia and New Zealand
James M. Kouzes, Barry Z. Posner with Michael Bunting

Lead with Wisdom
Mark Strom

The People Manager's Toolkit
Karen Gately

The New Rules of Management
Peter Cook

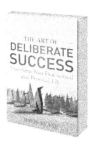

The Art of Deliberate Success
David Keane

Dealing with the Tough Stuff
Darren Hill, Alison Hill, Sean Richardson

First Be Nimble
Graham Winter

Available in print and e-book formats

WILEY